Marisa Agostini

Corporate Financial Distress

Going Concern Evaluation in Both International and U.S. Contexts

Marisa Agostini
Department of Management
Ca' Foscari University
Venice, Italy

ISBN 978-3-319-78499-1   ISBN 978-3-319-78500-4   (eBook)
https://doi.org/10.1007/978-3-319-78500-4

Library of Congress Control Number: 2018939951

Cover illustration: Cover pattern © Harvey Loake

Printed on acid-free paper

This Palgrave Pivot imprint is published by the registered company Springer International Publishing AG part of Springer Nature.
The registered company address is: Gewerbestrasse 11, 6330 Cham, Switzerland

PREFACE

The book aims at providing a panorama of the ongoing academic debate about corporate financial distress and the methods implemented to evaluate it by both managers and auditors in both international and US contexts. In particular, four main points will be investigated. First, a complete and in-depth consideration of corporate financial distress in academic debate aims to update the existing literature and provide new evidence. Second, the adopted perspective specifically focuses on going concern evaluation. This is usually considered together with other accounting or auditing assumptions, while this book emphasizes its individual relevance. Third, both accounting and auditing standards are examined according to the recent evolutions of both. They are usually analysed separately: this project considers going concern evaluations in relation to both international standards and US principles. Fourth, auditors' and managers' tools of evaluation and opinions are compared in terms of both affinities and differences. The present book, therefore, offers a complete overview of the concept of corporate financial distress, emphasizing the different typologies of corporate paths included in this broad concept. It reorganizes and updates academic literature about the evaluation of corporate financial distress (Altman and Hotchkiss 2010; Al-Hadi et al. 2017), from the first studies about failure prediction (Beaver 1966; Altman 1968; FitzPatrick 1932) to the most recent contributions (Koh et al. 2015; Donovan et al. 2015; Tinoco and Wilson 2013). Thus it brings together different streams of academic research, both accounting and auditing literature about going concern evaluation being reorganized around the common research field of corporate financial distress. The book provides evidence about the evolution of going concern standards in both international and US contexts. For this reason, it addresses different types of audience, including professionals (looking for categorization and definitions concerning the complex phenomenon of corporate financial distress and its evaluation), standard setters (considering the ongoing convergence process with regard to going concern evaluation), and students (being a research tool for doctoral students and a textbook for students of both financial accounting and auditing). In terms of organization, this book is divided into three main parts. The first introduces the complex phenomenon of corporate financial distress (Chap. 2), illustrating its articulation in different typologies of corporate path, reviewing definitions, and providing a re-assessment of the relevant academic literature. The book aims at relating together different streams of literature regarding and explaining bankruptcy, failure, and financial distress, focusing on both fraud and no-tort cases (i.e. true and fair representation in financial statements). Starting from this analysis, six corporate cases of corporate financial distress are identified and looked at closely. The second part focuses on the going concern evaluation of corporate financial distress in the US context, providing empirical evidence (Chap. 3). Special attention is devoted to the timeliness of going concern evaluations during severe corporate financial distress in both fraud and no-tort cases. The analysis also focuses on the importance of investigating cases of undetected fraud (concealing corporate financial distress), given the current lack of academic contributions and empirical evidence about them. This section also suggests some promising premises for future research. The third part analyses the reasons for, and development of, recent developments of US and international standards about going concern evaluation (Chap. 4). A final chapter reprises the set of research questions investigated in the book in order to summarize the overall argument in the concluding remarks and propose directions for future research (Chap. 5). The entire book emphasizes the role of time as an essential variable needing to be taken into account in the analysis of the entire corporate path characterized by financial distress. Going concern evaluation must be timely to be efficacious, as emphasized by the US investors' complaint recalled more than once in the course of this book. Time determines the difference between temporary and severe manifestations of financial distress, but it also bears on the restructuring of distressed companies because of the negative relation between prolongation of corporate financial corporate distress and the possibility of recovery.

Venice, Italy   Marisa Agostini

BIBLIOGRAPHY

Al-Hadi, A., Chatterjee, B., Yaftian, A., Taylor, G., & Monzur Hasan, M. (2017). Corporate social responsibility performance, financial distress and firm life cycle: Evidence from Australia. *Accounting & Finance.*

Altman, E. I. (1968). Financial ratios, discriminant analysis and the prediction of corporate bankruptcy. *The Journal of Finance, 23*(4), 589–609.

Altman, E. I., & Hotchkiss, E. (2010). *Corporate financial distress and bankruptcy: Predict and avoid bankruptcy, analyze and invest in distressed debt* (Vol. 289). John Wiley & Sons.

Beaver, W. H. (1966). Financial ratios as predictors of failure. *Journal of Accounting Research, 4,* 71–111.

Donovan, J., Frankel, R. M., & Martin, X. (2015). Accounting conservatism and creditor recovery rate. *The Accounting Review, 90*(6), 2267–2303.

FitzPatrick, P. J. (1932). A comparison of the ratios of successful industrial enterprises with those of failed companies. *Certified Public Accountant, 2,* 598–605.

Koh, S., Durand, R. B., Dai, L., & Chang, M. (2015). Financial distress: Lifecycle and corporate restructuring. *Journal of Corporate Finance, 33,* 19–33.

Tinoco, M. H., & Wilson, N. (2013). Financial distress and bankruptcy prediction among listed companies using accounting, market and macroeconomic variables. *International Review of Financial Analysis, 30,* 394–419.

ACKNOWLEDGEMENTS

First and foremost, I am grateful to professors Ugo Sostero and Erasmo Santesso for working with me and encouraging me to develop my own research agenda. I would also like to acknowledge professors Giovanni Favero, Stephen Limberg, Chiara Mio, Lee Parker, and Chiara Saccon for their constructive advice and comments at the beginning of this work.

Special thanks go to my colleagues at the Department of Management for their constant intellectual and emotional support, especially to Giulia Baschieri, Elisa Cavezzali, Francesca Checchinato, Caterina Cruciani, Gloria Gardenal, Maria Lusiani, Anna Moretti, and Alessandra Perri.

Finally, my deepest gratitude to my family, especially to my husband, for being a tower of strength, to my mother and mother-in-law for their irreplaceable support, and to my son and daughter for being a constant source of delight.

CONTENTS

1 Introduction   1

2 Corporate Financial Distress: A Roadmap of the Academic
  Literature Concerning its Definition and Tools
  of Evaluation   5

3 Going Concern Evaluation in the US Context:
  The Respective Roles of Auditors and Managers   49

4 The International Accounting Convergence Promoted by
  IASB and FASB Regarding Going Concern Status   99

5 The Role of Going Concern Evaluation in Both Prediction
  and Explanation of Corporate Financial Distress:
  Concluding Remarks and Future Trends   119

Index   127

LIST OF FIGURES

Fig. 3.1   Survival analyses for both *time1* and *time2* variables   62

Fig. 3.2   Survival analysis for both *time1* and *time2* variables
distinguishing between no-tort and fraud cases   62

Fig. 3.3   Survival analysis of the time between the fraud disclosure date
and the date of macro-failure   64

Fig. 3.4   Decision process to follow for evaluating whether there is
substantial doubt about an entity's ability to continue as a going
concern and determining related disclosure requirements
according to US generally accepted accounting principles
(Presentation of Financial Statements—Going Concern,
Subtopic 205-40)   89

LIST OF TABLES

Table 2.1   Micro-failure examples categorized according to the
            traditional clusters   17
Table 2.2   Schematization of six cases of corporate financial distress   18
Table 3.1   The investigated sample, including all the US fraud cases (and
            the matched no-tort cases) mentioned by the UCLA–LoPucki
            Bankruptcy Research Database, acting in a SIC code division
            different from the H and filing for bankruptcy between 1991
            and March 1, 2010   57
Table 3.2   Micro-failures categorization according to the traditional
            clusters   60
Table 3.3   Descriptive statistical analysis of *time1* and *time2* variables 62
Table 3.4   Descriptive statistical analysis of both *time2_fraud* and
            time3_fraud variables   63
Table 3.5   Descriptive statistical analysis of both *time2_notort* and
            time3_notort variables   63
Table 3.6   Relevant steps in Sunbeam Corp's path of financial distress   65
Table 3.7   Albert Dunlap's main working experiences   72
Table 3.8   Dunlap's dream management team in his different corporate
            experiences   75
Table 4.1   Chronology of the going concern assumption in the US
            context   106
Table 4.2   Going concern assumptions according to IFRS and US GAAP   112

CHAPTER 1

Introduction

Abstract The introduction provides a map of the entire book, which focuses on going concern evaluations of companies in financial distress. A complete overview of this corporate path is relevant for both academic debate and the professional world. The classification and updating of the existing academic literature allow us to highlight the key features, types, and signals of corporate financial distress. The evaluation of companies in financial distress and the respective roles of auditors and managers are explored first of all in the US context, where going concern assessment has for years been exclusively the responsibility of auditors. The book analyses the timing of going concern evaluation during corporate financial distress, in order to introduce the recent modifications of accounting and auditing standards in both US and international contexts.

Keywords Corporate financial distress • Corporate life cycle • Corporate risks • Corporate status • Firm failure

This book examines corporate financial distress, as a negative corporate status. The importance of focusing on negative corporate situations, rather than only on successful ones, has been emphasized by authoritative literature in the field (Sitkin 1992; McGrath 1999; Thornhill and Amit 2003). Specifically, corporate financial distress is still considered a vague term (Altman and Hotchkiss 2010) and related (in imprecise ways) to different

© The Author(s) 2018
M. Agostini, *Corporate Financial Distress*,
https://doi.org/10.1007/978-3-319-78500-4_1

terms such as failure and bankruptcy. This book aims at shedding some light on this state of affairs and also on such terminological distinctions. In particular, this study aims to back up "the view that there is value to be gained from the study of failed organizations. Just as medical science would be unlikely to progress by studying only healthy individuals, organization science may be limited in the knowledge attainable only from the study of successful firms. While these results shed new light on why firms fail at different ages, much remains to be learned about firm failure" (Thornhill and Amit 2003, p. 506). According to the concepts introduced and developed in the second chapter of this book, failure represents a specific type of corporate path in the experience of financial distress. A complete overview of this corporate path is relevant for both academic debate and the professional world. The classification and updating of the existing academic literature allow us to highlight recurring features, types, and signals of corporate financial distress (Koh et al. 2015). It does not coincide with precisely timed legal events, such as bankruptcy, because it represents a continuing corporate status. Its extension in time makes difficult its ex ante prediction through statistical methods because of difficulties in catching the complex dynamics of such processes in actual practice. After introducing the concept of corporate financial distress, the book analyses its causes, consequences, and timing. More than one step is identified in the path of financial distress, and the distinction between temporary and severe financial distress is introduced. The symptoms of both these types may be either truly and fairly represented in financial statements or fraudulently concealed. Such symptoms (or consequences) are financial ones (as highlighted by the term itself—'corporate financial distress'), but the causes and the corrective measures can be of different types, as pointed out in Chap. 2. Moreover, there is a relationship between corporate financial distress and managers' propensity to take on more risk (Edwards et al. 2013). Corporate financial distress, therefore, represents a negative lasting corporate status that implies risks and uncertainties for all the parties, both internal and external, who have an interest in the distressed company. The time factor is crucial. Authoritative literature has emphasized the relation between the increase in the time of corporate paths of financial distress and the costs of the default, the already noted managers' propensity to embark on risky reactive initiatives, and the difficulties of corporate recovery. These difficulties also influence the end result of the corporate path of financial distress: recovery is possible after a temporary distress, while a case of severe financial distress entails a failing process leading to either bankruptcy or another major mutation (e.g. merger, absorption, dissolution, liquidation, etc.). The analysis implemented in the following chapters also points to an order of preference for distressed entities regarding such final events. This observation is made possible by a full consideration of the time variable, entailing a change of focus beyond mere prediction towards an explanation of corporate financial distress. The present book first analyses the progressive development of statistical prediction models, from univariate discriminant analysis to artificial intelligent systems and from bankruptcy prediction to the assessment of corporate financial distress. These are all static modelling prediction tools. The next chapter highlights both their drawbacks and their possible uses. Such considerations go some way towards explaining the progressive shift of academic focus from mere prediction to fuller evaluations of corporate financial distress. Traditionally, prediction and explanation have been kept separate: this book proposes to apply both together. The evaluation of distressed companies and the respective roles of auditors and managers are firstly explored in the US context (Chap. 3). Here, the going concern assessment has for years been the auditors' responsibility, but investors have complained that by the time auditors make their assessment, a deteriorating business is on the verge of bankruptcy or a delisting from its stock exchange. The book aims to empirically verify this complaint in order to introduce recent developments in updating accounting and auditing standards in the US. These changes relate to the converging process being implemented by International Accounting Standards Board (IASB) and Financial Accounting Standards Board (FASB) regarding going concern assumptions with a view to overcoming substantial and potentially problematic differences between international standards and US principles. The present work (Chap. 4) considers this project of convergence and the applied statements in both (US and international) contexts.

BIBLIOGRAPHY

Altman, E. I., & Hotchkiss, E. (2010). *Corporate financial distress and bankruptcy: Predict and avoid bankruptcy, analyze and invest in distressed debt* (Vol. 289). Hoboken, NJ: John Wiley & Sons.

Edwards, A., Schwab, C., & Shevlin, T. (2013, February). Financial constraints and the incentive for tax planning. In *2013 American Taxation Association mid-year meeting: New faculty/doctoral student session* (Vol. 2216875). Retrieved October 6, 2017, from http://papers.ssrn.com/abstract

Koh, S., Durand, R. B., Dai, L., & Chang, M. (2015). Financial distress: Lifecycle and corporate restructuring. *Journal of Corporate Finance, 33*, 19–33.

McGrath, R. G. (1999). Falling forward: Real options reasoning and entrepreneurial failure. *Academy of Management Review, 24*(1), 13–30.

Sitkin, S. B. (1992). Learning through failure: The strategy of small losses. *Research in Organizational Behavior, 14*, 231–266.

Thornhill, S., & Amit, R. (2003). Learning about failure: Bankruptcy, firm age, and the resource-based view. *Organization Science, 14*(5), 497–509.

CHAPTER 2

Corporate Financial Distress: A Roadmap of the Academic Literature Concerning its Definition and Tools of Evaluation

Abstract Global financial crises have emphasized the importance of understanding current and future corporate financial states. A literature review about financial distress permits us to define it independently from the financial nature of its causes: companies may also face financial distress as a consequence of non-financial factors characterizing its starting point. After this initial step, a firm may either recover its financial situation (temporary distress) or embark on a failure path (severe financial distress). Both these cases may correspond to either a no tort or a fraud (either disclosed or undetected). The cases examined here are also relevant for understanding the passage of the focus of academic debate from prediction to explanation in order to minutely examine how companies mutate from successful into distressed ones.

Keywords Auditors • Bankruptcy • Corporate financial distress • Failure prediction • Undetected fraud

2.1 Financial Distress: Definition and Main Features

Since first devoting its attention to the subject, academic literature has emphasized the *difficulties in defining* corporate financial distress because of the incomplete and arbitrary nature of any criteria by which to classify

© The Author(s) 2018
M. Agostini, *Corporate Financial Distress*,
https://doi.org/10.1007/978-3-319-78500-4_2

it (Keasey and Watson 1991). There is no consensus on how financial distress affects corporate performance, but it is costly (Opler and Titman 1994) and needs to be investigated. Altman (1993) relates corporate financial distress to unsuccessful business enterprise and defines four generic terms that are commonly used in the literature about it: failure, insolvency, bankruptcy, and default.[1] Corporate financial distress remains, none the less, a vague term (Altman and Hotchkiss 2006) that does not correspond to an absolute condition such as bankruptcy or insolvency (Sun et al. 2016). This chapter aims at shedding some light on the matter.

Corporate financial distress identifies a status that is extended in time, *embracing the failure path* and (both possibly and ultimately) the event of bankruptcy. Default prediction literature has traditionally been focused on highly visible legal events that characterize the end of a firm's life cycle and that can be objectively and accurately dated. On the one hand, such events can be precisely defined and identified. Bankruptcy constitutes an everyday example of a legal event characterizing the end of a firm life cycle. Its likelihood can be represented using binary choice models where the populations of failing and non-failing firms are separated from each other in a precise (and therefore artificial) way on the basis of a specifically chosen time period (Altman and Eisenbeis 1978; Balcaen and Ooghe 2006; Ooghe and Verbaere 1985; Ooghe and Joos 1990; Ooghe et al. 1995;

---

[1] These four terms (i.e. failure, insolvency, default, and bankruptcy) are sometimes used interchangeably even though they have distinct formal usages (Altman 1993; Altman and Hotchkiss 2006, 2010).

Failure has been defined as the persistent lower value of the realized rate of return on invested capital than the same rate on equivalent investments.

Insolvency, and in particular "technical insolvency", is a term referring to the status in which unsuccessful firms are unable to meet their current liabilities. This status could be a temporary one but it can be immediately transformed into the reason for declaring bankruptcy. If the status is chronic instead of temporary, it is defined as "insolvency in the bankruptcy sense". In this case the evaluation concerns the total liabilities on a fair valuation of the total assets in which the liabilities assume higher value than the total assets.

Another term concerning a firm's distress condition is *default*. It can be technical and/or legal. The technical default refers to the condition in which the debtor firm violates a condition of an agreement. Consequently, the status evolves in legal default when the creditor takes legal action against the debtor. However, legal default is rare since a renegotiation is often adopted with the agreement of the two firms.

Finally, *bankruptcy* refers to the condition in which the firm is declared bankrupt in a federal district court through a petition aiming to liquidate its assets (Chap. 7) or trying to implement a recovery programme (Chap. 11) in the US context.

Frydman et al. 1985; Theodossiou et al. 1996; Blocher et al. 1999). On the other hand (and more pertinently to this work), such a legal event does not sufficiently represent the *real-economic complexity* of corporate paths through financial distress. For instance, if an unsuccessful firm passes through a lengthy failing process, there will be a considerable time gap between the period that a firm enters a state of financial distress and the possible final event of legal bankruptcy (Balcaen and Ooghe 2006). The consideration of financial distress as a path (instead of an event) appears more complex to precisely define and categorize, but closer to the reality because it does not consider only the legal date of a final event. This consideration requires us to identify and date different steps in the corporate process characterized by financial distress: extension in time makes it a sequence of steps instead of a single freeze-frame event (Agostini 2013). In this way, financial distress becomes a *dynamic process* where the majority of distressed firms do not actually become bankrupt.

Recognition of the fact that corporate failure does not lead inevitably to a filing for bankruptcy has been gaining ground in academic literature and has been the essential premise for the evolution of the definition of financial distress after the initial contributions to the topic (Jones 1987; Gilbert et al. 1990; Flagg et al. 1991; Barnes 1987; Barnes 1990). Both academic and practitioners' studies try to move from ex post models to *ex ante approaches* while remaining based on financial symptoms of corporate distress. These newer approaches adopt financial criteria based on corporate failure to meet financial obligations and consider a firm as financially distressed not only when it files for bankruptcy (Wruck 1990; Asquith et al. 1994; Andrade and Kaplan 1998; Whitaker 1999; Sanz and Ayca 2006). Flagg et al. (1991) were among the first to consider a sample of exclusively distressed firms and identify four events (i.e. reductions in dividends, "going concern" qualified opinions, troubled debt restructurings, and violations of debt covenants) signalling that a firm is experiencing financial distress. Chen et al. (1995) were then among the first to define distress as the condition where a firm's liquidation of total assets is less than the total value of creditor claims. If prolonged, this situation can lead to forced liquidation or bankruptcy; for this reason, financial distress is often referred to as the likelihood of bankruptcy, which is dependent on the availability of liquidity and credit (Hendel 1996). Pindado et al. (2008) introduces a dynamic proxy of corporate financial distress that is independent of the (final) outcome (e.g. bankruptcy) while still based only on financial symptoms. This approach classifies a company as financially distressed whenever its operational cash flows are lower than financial expenses and market value persistently falls. Focusing on the early stages of financial distress, rather than predicting an eventual bankruptcy, has progressively become a prime concern of the academic literature.

The role of *time extension* is a significant recognition (Balcaen and Ooghe 2006), but still represents only a first step forward for defining corporate financial distress. Such distress implies a lengthened pathological condition for firms in which the term "financial" describes its main consequences. Therefore, corporate financial distress can be defined as a negative lasting situation during which a firm experiences bad financial conditions such as low liquidity, inability to pay debts, restriction on dividend distribution policy, increase in the cost of capital, reduction in access to external funding sources, and weaker credit ratings. Academic literature provides several examples of such *financial consequences* represented as negative (financial) accounting items, and these have been used as criteria in financial distress definitions. The most frequent examples are several years of negative net operating income, suspension of dividend payments, major restructuring or layoffs (Platt and Platt 2002), low interest coverage ratio, negative earnings before interest and taxes (EBIT), negative net income before special items, losses, selling shares to private investors, successive years of negative shareholders' funds or accumulated losses (McLeay and Omar 2000), an increase in the cost of capital, a reduction in access to external funding sources, and weaker credit ratings. The negative consequences deriving from financial distress can be also differentiated according to *the stage of enterprise life cycle*. According to life cycle theory, growing capacity, access to resources, and strategies vary during a firm's life cycle (Anthony and Ramesh 1992), which consists of four stages: birth, growth, maturity, and decline. In the early stages of its growth, firms are typically small, dominated by their owners (entrepreneurs), simple, informal in structure, undifferentiated, and with highly centralized power systems and considerable focus on innovation (Miller and Friesen 1984). Inevitably, these firms face significant uncertainty over future growth, which is manifested in higher book-to-market ratios and greater firm-specific risk (Pastor and Veronesi 2003). Corporate financial distress in the birth stage is usually related to deficiency of liquidity or cash flow difficulty (Spence 1977, 1979, 1981; Jenkins et al. 2004; Hasan et al. 2015). In the second stage, as the name suggests (i.e. growing period), firms may achieve rapid growth, acquire new (multiple) shareholders, and gain separation between ownership and control with managers assuming more decision-making responsibility (Miller and Friesen 1984; Mueller 1972). In the growing period, corporate financial distress is usually related to excessive financial leverage because of the perceived need to expand capital. In the last stages of the enterprise life cycle, firms are less prone to innovation and risky strategies than in their birth and growth stages. In particular, mature firms aim for the smooth functioning of the business in a well-defined market (Miller and Friesen 1984), while firms in decline aim to collect as much revenue from existing operations as possible (Thietart and Vivas 1984), in the face of encroaching stagnation and low profitability (Miller and Friesen 1984). This focus on enterprise life cycle confirms that corporate conditions measured through financial accounting items are contingent on different firms' features and behaviours at different stages.

According to life cycle theory, *corrective measures and restructuring strategies* adopted by firms facing corporate financial distress can also be of different types and may be conditioned by the firm's stage in the corporate life cycle (Koh et al. 2015). Indeed, while some strategies have an association with recovery for all firms regardless of where they are in the life cycle (such as reducing investment and dividends), there is some evidence concerning the interaction of life cycle and the choice of other specific restructuring strategies. For instance, firms facing corporate financial distress in the earlier stages of their life cycle have a tendency to reduce their employees, while mature distressed firms are more likely to engage in asset restructuring. Koh et al. (2015) invite companies facing financial distress to adopt at least (and ideally not more than) three strategies to attempt recovery. In any case, there is no guarantee that the implemented strategies will be effective in rescuing the firm from financial distress, not least because of potentially inappropriate managerial reactions to signals that a firm is experiencing distress. In particular, such negative persisting conditions and their possible consequences may increase managers' propensity to *take on more risk*. For instance, Edwards et al. (2013) emphasize the increase in managers' disposition to seek additional cash in order to finance corporate existing operations and improve corporate solvency—an increase related to the possible emergence of the consequences of financial distress and to an ultimate attempt to forestall (sometimes to hide) unfavourable signals. These are considered deeply discrediting for top management's image: an organization's poor performance implies that its leader is not competent and unable to achieve organizational success (Sutton and Callahan 1987). These negative feelings both threaten managerial careers and increase the probability of organizational demise. They worsen corporate financial distress with the consequence that financial distress can become seriously costly for *several parties*, especially for creditors. Since the initial focus on corporate financial distress, academic research has emphasized the conflicts of interest between borrowers and lenders (Jensen and Meckling 1976; Myers 1977; Stulz 1990), between firms and their non-financial stakeholders (Baxter 1967; Titman 1984; Maksimovic and Titman 1991), and between shareholders and managers (Gilson and Vetsuypens 1993; Novaes and Zingales 1993). Corporate financial distress creates a tendency for firms to do things that are harmful to several parties, impairing access to credit and raising the cost of stakeholder relationships (Opler and Titman 1994). Studies of corporate distress have mostly focused on these financial consequences because they represent signals of firms' lasting negative states. Samples of firms that might be considered to be in distress have been created by examination of various markers: Lau (1987) and Hill et al. (1996) use layoffs, restructurings, or missed dividend payments; Asquith et al. (1994) allow an interest coverage ratio to define distress; similarly, Whitaker (1999) measures distress as the first year in which cash flow is less than current maturities of long-term debt; and John et al. (1992) let the change in equity price define distress. The problem with these indicators is that some companies displaying these signals may not actually be in distress. Layoffs may occur in specific divisions of otherwise healthy enterprises, restructurings may occur at different stages of decline, and there are many explanations for missed dividend payments (Platt and Platt 2002). Academic default literature generally focuses on financial signals and symptoms (Beynon and Peel 2001; Dimitras et al. 1999; Ooghe et al. 1995; Pompe and Bilderbeek 2005), but it examines only a limited number of non-financial causes and specific types of enterprises (Ooghe and De Prijcker 2008; Everett and Watson 1998; Charan et al. 2002; Hambrick and D'Aveni 1992). It typically emphasizes the scarce availability of financial resources, but it does not explore alternative *causes* to such financial factors. Indeed, firms may enter financial distress as the result of economic distress, a decline in the firm's industry as a whole, poor management (Wruck 1990), and/or other reasons. Financial distress may be the result of both internal and external factors bearing on the enterprise. Companies may also face financial distress as a consequence of non-financial factors (Sun and Li 2011). This also explains why different corrective measures may be required in order to exit the distressed status. Financial consequences of corporate distress may also derive from non-financial factors, but the symptoms of such distress only become evident from a firm's solvency and financial conditions.

> Such distress includes various conditions, such as low liquidity, inability to pay debts or dividend of preference stock, substantial and continual reduction in profitability, and bankruptcy. These conditions indicate financial distress from mild to serious in sequence. Financial distress is the synthetic reflection of deterioration of inner and outside risky factors of an enterprise. Even enterprise distress caused by non-financial factors tends to end up with financial distress (Sun and Li 2011, p. 2566).

Non-financial outside risky factors are, for instance, related to macroeconomic variables and to risk transfer along the supply chain. The transfer of financial distress risk from customers to suppliers is a hot matter of discussion in academic debate. It is particularly evident when distressed major customers influence their suppliers' financial distress in addition to the accounting- and market-based situation of the firm itself. Because of a linked firm's financial distress, rivals, customers, and suppliers can suffer feedback effects. Such reactive consequences have traditionally been examined only in relation to bankruptcy, starting from Lang and Stulz's work (1992). This investigates the effects of bankruptcy announcements (Chap. 11 filings) on the equity value of a firm's competitors. Such effects can be either positive (i.e. "competitive effects") or negative ("contagion effects"): on average, industry rivals suffer contagion effects around the time that a competitor files for bankruptcy. Several studies have been devoted to bankruptcy and its intra-industry contagion effects (Ferris et al. 1997; Hertzel and Smith 1993; Kang and Stulz 2000; Slovin et al. 1999). More recently, the analysis of such effects has also focused on distressed companies, suggesting that financial distress has broad, even economy-wide effects. In particular, Hertzel et al. (2008) highlight significant pre-filing and filing-date contagion effects affecting industry rivals and extending beyond industry competitors along the supply chain to suppliers of the filing firms. "In discussions of the trade-off theory, the actions of suppliers and customers of firms in distress are often cited as a source of indirect costs that can arise with impending bankruptcy. Suppliers can impose costs on distressed firms by failing to supply trade credit, backing away from entering into long-term contracts, or delaying shipments. Customers, wary of product quality, reduced value of warranties, continuity of supply, and serviceability, impose costs by shifting purchases to existing and/or new suppliers" (Hertzel et al. 2008, p. 375). Because of contagion effects, there can be the shift from corporate financial distress (which is firm-specific distress) to economic distress that is industry-wide. Moreover, suppliers' contagion effects are more severe when the intra-industry competitors of the filing firm also suffer contagion. More recently, Kolay et al. (2016) studied the nature of "spillover effects" of corporate financial distress on rivals, suppliers, and customers. Finally, Lian (2017) focuses on whether and how risks transfer along the supply chain, specifically examining the impact of distressed major customers on the probability of suppliers' financial distress in the future. Corporate financial distress down the line may thus originate because of such contagion effects: its causes may be of various types and not only financial factors.

An impediment in the widespread dissemination of research about corporate financial distress is the lack of a precise categorization of such causes and a consistent definition of *when companies enter such paths*. This has been collocated in a "grey area", that is, the area of overlap or indecisive area that separates surviving from risky firms (Cybinski 2001). Thus, corporate financial distress represents a continuum to be investigated with predominantly explanatory objectives aimed at detecting signals of a firm's deteriorating condition over time. This "grey area" is particularly difficult to classify, but it is also of particular interest. The analysis requires a comparison of each distressed firm with itself over time, to understand how firms transform from successful ones into failed ones. Thus, the identification of the beginning of the stage of corporate distress requires the analysis of its causes. This emphasizes the association between financial distress and *ERM*, that is, Enterprise Risk Management (Hoyt and Liebenberg 2011; Beasley et al. 2015). The most widely accepted ERM framework has been developed by COSO (2004) and defines ERM as follows: "Enterprise risk management is a process, effected by an entity's board of directors, management and other personnel, applied in a strategy setting and across the enterprise, designed to identify potential events that may affect the entity, and manage risk to be within its risk appetite, to provide reasonable assurance regarding the achievement of the entity's objectives." The global financial crisis that began in 2008 emphasized the shortcomings of existing risk management practices and stressed the importance of the concept of financial distress that becomes central for ERM (Cohen et al. 2017; Asare et al. 2012; Baxter et al. 2013; Kaplan and Mikes 2013). Companies in financial distress have lower-quality ERM programmes, probably due to resource constraints inhibiting the investment necessary for effective ERM

(Baxter et al. 2013). This also contributes to explaining the lack of focus on the causes of corporate financial distress. Only a focus on such causes will allow us to adopt an ex ante approach (Pindado et al. 2008) that can be applied regardless of financial consequences and final outcome (e.g. bankruptcy).

Summarizing, this paragraph suggests that corporate financial distress is an extended pathological condition whose financial consequences have been explored in depth by academic studies. Recent contributions differentiate its symptoms and the corrective measures according to the stage of the enterprise life cycle. On the other hand, the analysis of its causes is more difficult because these may be of different types (including non-financial factors). This has been recently emphasized by studies investigating the association between corporate financial distress and ERM. The main problem seems to be related to the lack of a consistent definition of exactly when companies embark on a path of financial distress. From a temporal point of view, corporate financial distress may prove an ongoing condition that could include a failure path and (both possibly and ultimately) bankruptcy.

2.2 Financial Distress and Corporate Failure

Traditionally, academic research has focused on corporate failure, making it coincident with bankruptcy for predicting purposes. As recalled in the previous paragraph, recent authoritative literature (Altman and Hotchkiss 2006) states that corporate financial distress is still a vague term that can be related to four other generic terms: failure, insolvency, bankruptcy, and default. This implies a continuing degree of uncertainty about its analysis. This paragraph starts by considering bankruptcy in order to distinguish it from corporate failure and financial distress. All three phenomena will be investigated in order to emphasize both their common features and their differences.

Failure and bankruptcy have for a long time been considered interchangeable terms, defining the first as receivership, voluntary liquidation (creditors), winding up by court order, or equivalent (Taffler 1982). The same has been done for corporate financial distress considering that, within a given year, a firm is financially distressed if it is in default on its debt, bankrupt, or privately restructuring its debt to avoid bankruptcy (Gilson 1989). Progressively, the status of unsuccessful firms has been more precisely categorized to determine what financial state category each firm falls into, from least to most distressed (Lau 1987). This has led to the recognition that there are several stages that a firm can go through before it is defined as dead, such as financial distress, insolvency, filing for bankruptcy, and administrative receivership to avoid filing for bankruptcy (Wruck 1990). Consideration of the *time variable* has shown that firms tend to stop providing accounts some years before the bankruptcy filing (Theodossiou 1993). The implication is that such firms are already in serious financial distress at some point before the legal bankruptcy event. In this way bankruptcy has been identified as a legal event precisely dated in time. This explains why there is abundant literature describing prediction models of corporate bankruptcy. It is an event that is definitive and clearly identifiable. For instance, in the US context, firms are considered bankrupt when a petition is filed under either Chap. 11 or Chap. 7 of the US Bankruptcy Code. However, under Chap. 11, a firm's impaired debts are replaced by new financial claims, on the assumption that the firm will be reorganized; under Chap. 7, the firm is liquidated.[2] As an alternative to the formal court-supervised bankruptcy process, firms and their creditors can also privately agree to restructure troubled debt.

Starting from these premises, Platt and Platt (2002) underline that financial distress is a late stage of corporate decline that precedes more cataclysmic events such as bankruptcy or liquidation. Therefore, bankruptcy is a legal event that corresponds to a specific type of default. It is only one possibility of macro-failure, that is, the last stage of a firm's life cycle that represents an important type of discontinuance, requiring a defensive reaction (i.e. a *radical change*) in the firm that wants to survive (Agostini 2013). Moreover, it represents a more limited concept than financial distress (Pindado et al. 2008). While bankruptcy is an event precisely dated in time, failure and financial distress represent corporate paths that are extended in time. Both these paths precede the possible eventual bankruptcy. Few researchers have explicitly analysed corporate failure as a process (Ooghe and De Prijcker 2008) even after the recognition that it cannot be connected to a well-defined dichotomous variable. The oldest and most well-known exception is Argenti (1976), relating non-financial failure causes with financial indicators within three different failure pro-

---

[2] There are also other alternative chapters of the US Bankruptcy Code, which are not considered here (given also the specific sample analysed in the third chapter). Indeed, the Bankruptcy Reform Act of 1978 was divided into four titles and the first title (known as "the code") was divided into eight chapters: 1, 3, 5, 7, 9, 11, 13, 15. The Bankruptcy Reform Act of 1978 has been amended several times since, with the most significant recent changes enacted in 2005 through BAPCPA 2005.

cesses. Altman (1984) is among the first to emphasize that the failure to meet financial obligations does not necessarily lead to bankruptcy.

The analysis of corporate financial distress is of more recent vintage, although academic literature has emphasized for some time the need to monitor corporate financial distress in ways that do not necessarily entail the prediction of the event of bankruptcy (Barnes 1987, 1990). The lack of work on this matter is in part related to the difficulty in defining objectively the onset of financial distress. By contrast, the bankruptcy date is definitive and financial data prior to that date are reasonably accessible. Because of the indeterminacy of when a firm becomes financially distressed, most research that purports to study financial distress instead examines the terminal date associated with the company's filing for bankruptcy protection (Platt and Platt 2002). So, a common feature between corporate failure and financial distress regards *the extension in time.* They are often considered synonyms because they both stress a continuous difficulty in being able to meet liabilities as they became due and are the sources of a costly process which can be overcome by restructuring and do not (necessarily) imply bankruptcy (Keasey et al. 2015). There is still a degree of confusion in the academic literature about the common traits, and more especially the differences, between the concepts of financial distress and failure. Platt and Platt (2002) emphasize that the distress stage of companies is serious but not fatal. They specify that the given description is inexact, including companies whose troubles exceed the early-stage symptoms of negative EBIT, net income, or cash flow. They focus on the financial symptoms experienced by distressed companies that have had trouble paying their own suppliers, have missed payments to their bank, or may have difficulty servicing the next payroll. Further, most have sustained net losses for several years or have suspended dividend payments in an effort to marshal financial resources to deal with operational or debt-related problems. In the absence of intervention, it is likely that most, if not all, of these firms would eventually move on to failure and file for bankruptcy protection. But firms may either fail or experience some other less severe form of financial distress. There is some evidence that firms experiencing less severe forms of financial distress can be distinguished from failed firms. Koh et al. (2015) measure financial distress according to firm's distance-to-default: a falling distance corresponds to default; an increasing distance indicates that firms are less likely to default or that they are recovering.

Starting from these premises, in the present work corporate financial distress is considered a *lasting negative corporate status that precedes in time the beginning of the failing path.* Indeed, after experiencing financial distress, a firm may either recover or enter the failing path that will ultimately imply a macro-failure such as the event of bankruptcy. So, the temporal dimension distinguishes the event of bankruptcy from the paths of corporate financial distress and failure. These are not synonyms because of their *possible different outcomes*: recovery is possible only after corporate financial distress, while only macro-failure characterizes the end of a failing path. Academic and practitioners' studies agree about the importance of focusing on corporate financial distress, which starts before failure, but it is difficult to identify the point at which a firm becomes distressed. *The starting point* of corporate financial distress is the stage of not meeting certain objectives due to enterprise actions or inactions that impact on profit (because of sales and expenses variations) which is liable to cause financial consequences in terms of solvency and liquidity (because of debt and cash flow variations). Its identification requires in-depth knowledge of the specific company and great attention towards "special signals" that can be of various types (not only financial) as listed and explained in this paragraph. Academic research that underlines non-financial factors as causes of default is very fragmented (e.g. Baum and Mezias 1992; Daily and Dalton 1995; Greening and Johnson 1996; Swaminathan 1996). Despite this fragmentation, most studies relate corporate default to managerial errors. Altman and Hotchkiss (2010) emphasize that firms fail for a multiplicity of reasons, but managerial inadequacies represent the core of corporate problems in most of the cases. Ooghe and De Prijcker (2008) implement a case study research based on companies of different industries, sizes, and ages that, in the end, fall into bankruptcy. They identify four different types of failure processes and, for each process, provide a detailed overview of the direct and indirect effects of non-financial and financial causes. Their work emphasizes that precise identification of causes and initial stages of corporate financial distress require in-depth investigation and the acquisition of knowledge about the specific corporate case through a qualitative method (such as case study research) to explain factors, signals, and symptoms. This approach has been applied for the identification and examination of firms' actions (or inactions) and *the consequent missed objectives*, known as micro-failures (Agostini 2013). If a micro-failure occurs, a set business objective has become unattainable and the firm is experiencing a situation of financial distress. As the name emphasizes, this will have financial consequences in terms of liquidity because of variations in debt and cash flow. Great attention should therefore be paid to different types of micro-failures that are not atypical (Agostini 2013) and can be categorized according to the traditional clusters considered in the academic literature (Argenti 1976; Altman 1993). Several examples of micro-failures can be related to product/market, financial, managerial/key employee, cultural/social, and accidental problems (Table 2.1). There may then be both financial and non-financial factors as anticipated above.

Table 2.1 Micro-failure examples categorized according to the traditional clusters

---

A. *Product/market problems*
  A1. Competition and/or competitors with significantly greater financial resources than the company
  A2. Customers' criticism because of goods quality (either too expensive or too low quality)
  A3. Depressed industry and market downturn
  A4. New and stricter industry regulations
  A5. Seasonal business
B. *Financial problems*
  B1. Excessive costs and/or additional and non-essential expenses
  B2. Excessive indebtedness and difficulty in obtaining new financing
  B3. Investors' nervousness, bad relationship with the venture capitalists, and/or creditors' pressure
  B4. Negative economic/financial trends (primarily a decrease in revenues)
  B5. Relationship of strong financial dependence on other player(s) (suppliers, customers, ...)
  B6. Unprofitable ventures (e.g. acquisition of unprofitable divisions)
C. *Managerial/key employee problems*
  C1. Conflicts of interest
  C2. Core business abandonment and diversification into other industries
  C3. Excessive anxiety to keep up with increasingly large competitors
  C4. Important decisions made without obtaining board approval
  C5. Legal, apparently correct but improper (e.g. deficit analytical) accountancy
  C6. Poor management and disengaged board
  C7. Principals' legal problems unconnected with the firm
  C8. Private benefits (withdrawals, bonuses, and compensation policy)
  C9. Too aggressive growth and expansion strategy (i.e. rapid growth through mergers or other operations proving unsustainable in the long run)
  C10. Too ambitious objectives and anxiety to hit "must make" figures (i.e. earnings targets)
  C11. Mistaken operations (because of riskiness or other reasons)
D. *Cultural/social factors*
  D1. Corruption
  D2. Discrimination problems
  D3. Powerful enemies
E. *Accidental factors*
  E1. Calamities

Table 2.2   Schematization of six cases of corporate financial distress

		Corporate financial distress	
		Temporary	Severe
Presentation in financial statements	True and fair	Case 1	Case 3
	Disclosed fraud	Case 5[a]	Case 4
	Undetected fraud	Case 2	Case 6[a]

[a]To be empirically verified

After (at least one) micro-failure, a firm may either recover its financial situation where the distress is *temporary* (Donovan et al. 2015; Zhang 2008) or embark on a failure path because of *severe* financial distress. Therefore, corporate financial distress includes two alternative types of consequences, that is, a successful recovery or a failure path. Either case may correspond to a no tort (when there is a true and fair representation of the corporate situation in financial statements) or to a fraud situation which may be either disclosed or undetected. Thus, six alternative cases (Table 2.2) can be identified and analysed inside the broad concept of corporate financial distress. The differentiation between such cases is based on two criteria, that is, the type of financial distress (either temporary or severe) and its presentation in financial statements (either true and fair or incomplete in case of both detected and undetected fraud). Concerning *the type of corporate financial distress* (i.e. the first criterion), restructuring plays an important role for distressed firms and may be decisive for making a situation of financial distress either temporary or severe. When a firm, after a micro-failure, recognizes that it has entered on a condition of financial distress, it is vital that it respond immediately by taking corrective measures to enhance efficiency and control costs. Denis and Kruse (2000) find that, in such cases, firms' restructuring is associated with positive abnormal returns. However, the ability to engage in a strategy does not necessarily ensure a successful turnaround, which will depend more on the firm's ability to change its strategy, structure, and ideology than on restructuring based on short-term efficiency or cost-cutting tactics (Barker and Duhaime 1997). In particular, Sudarsanam and Lai (2001) provide four classifications of restructuring: managerial, operational, asset, and financial. Another variable that seems to be relevant in the distinction between temporary and severe financial distress is related to corporate governance attributes. So, for instance, the level of financial distress is reduced in the presence of both greater levels of director and blockholder ownership and the existence of a board audit committee (Miglani et al. 2015); outside directors and ownership by outside directors (Elloumi and Gueyle 2001); non-executive director ownership and the presence of outside blockholders (Nahar Abdullah 2006). Also, in these cases, time represents an essential variable to take into account for restructuring analysis and for preventing temporary financial distress from becoming severe. Academic research has suggested this point about failure: rapid reorganization leads to efficient bankruptcies. Jensen (1991) writes: "It often takes years to resolve individual cases. As a result of such delays, much of the operating value of businesses can be destroyed." For instance, the Bankruptcy Abuse Prevention and Consumer Protection Act (BAPCPA) of 2005 contains elements specifically designed to expedite bankruptcies (Covitz et al. 2006). The reason may be that the direct costs of restructuring (such as fees for retaining investment bankers, attorneys, and restructuring professionals) increase with time. Consistent with this view, Thorburn (2000) finds that the costs of bankruptcy increase with the time in default. Acharya et al. (2007) likewise find a statistically significant negative relationship between bond recovery rates and the time spent in default. Shorter failing paths also reduce the indirect costs by limiting the bankruptcy's impact on business reputation, freeing management from drawn-out negotiations, and reducing the extent to which firms forgo investment opportunities. Therefore, if the time variable is not seriously considered as essential for restructuring, and financial distress is prolonged, such situations can become severe (entering a failure path) and ultimately lead to macro-failure (Agostini 2013). This is the last stage of a firm's life cycle and represents an important type of discontinuance that requires a defensive reaction (i.e. a radical change) in the firm that wants to survive. This occurs after a process which evolves over a period of time, so it does not occur suddenly. There has been a recent increase in empirical studies exploring *entrepreneurial exit* (Wennberg and DeTienne 2014). Balcaen et al. (2012) examine three types of exit, demonstrating that following distress most companies either exit through bankruptcy or are voluntarily liquidated, while only a relatively small number are acquired, merged, or split. This is one of the reasons for which financial distress is often referred to as the likelihood of bankruptcy and related to the availability of liquidity and credit (Hendel 1996). In such cases, corporate financial distress is resolved either inside or outside the bankruptcy court. In the US, bankruptcy resolves impaired contractual claims against the firm through either liquidation (Chap. 7) or reorganization (Chap. 11). This allows the firm to continue operating while seeking to satisfy creditor claims. Bankruptcy is only one type of macro-failure: merger, absorption, dissolution, or liquidation are all alternatives. Indeed, when a firm begins to experience financial difficulties and there is a real possibility that it will fail, it should evaluate several possible alternatives such as a refinancing package, a restructuring of its assets, a change in the scale or scope of its operations, or a merger with another firm (Balcaen and Ooghe 2006). On the one hand, the type of macro-failure is surely related to the timeliness of the adopted strategy for restructuring as explained above: the financial consequences of corporate financial distress imply the worsening of corporate status and decide the specific distressed path of the company. On the other hand, much depends upon the economic interests and power of the different stakeholders who may continue to support distressed firms. For instance, bankers, creditors, and so on, whose actions may determine firms' paths, may eventually decide that a firm's financial condition and prospects are insufficient to justify continued support. This issue is strictly related to the corporate decision of disclosing (or not) financial distress.

Concerning *presentation in financial statements* (i.e. the second criterion), distressed companies may decide to either disclose their negative status or implement a fraud. Fraudulent financial reporting is defined as "an intentional misstatement of financial statements" (Arens et al. 2003) and it is the opposite of a fair presentation, where the flexibility within accounting is used to give a true and fair picture of the accounts so that they serve the interests of users. There is also another intermediate practice: creative accounting is implemented where the flexibility within accounting practice is exploited to manage the measurement and presentation of the accounts so that they serve the interests of preparers (Jones 2011). Such modes of presentation correlate to possible and different levels of use and misuse of accounting by managers. In the case of fraud there is the deliberate management decision of stepping outside the regulatory framework to give a false picture of the accounts (Jones 2011). Many cases of financial statement fraud may also stay undetectable. If a fraud remains undetected, only the fraudster himself or herself knows that a violation has taken place. The principals, on the other hand, remain unaware of their loss due to the fraud and therefore do not make the necessary adjustments to prevent future losses. This is also related to the type of macro-failure. Academic research has long investigated the relation between corporate financial distress and merger/acquisition. Peel and Wilson (1989) indicate that a significantly larger minority of merged firms (around 15–17% in their study) exhibits symptoms of financial distress in the year prior to merger than does the general population of firms (less than 5% are defined as distressed). Moreover, Peel (1990) suggests that it is usually the distressed firm which actively seeks a partner. These studies represent the premise for the investigation implemented in this book. Merger and acquisition represent a type of macro-failure for distressed companies that appears preferable to other alternatives. Given the definition of fraud provided above, it is usually kept hidden by companies. The so-called linkage problem identifies fraudsters' fear of being discovered if the fraud ceases, because of a higher probability of uncovering fraud in such a case (Baer 2008). For this reason, the macro-failure category becomes relevant and a sort of rating of managers' preferences about macro-failure can be considered. In particular, managers may prefer to resort to lobbying (Yu and Yu 2011) or to mergers and acquisitions (Erickson et al. 2011) as a means to postpone or avoid fraud disclosure.

The two described criteria (i.e. the varieties of corporate financial distress and its representation in financial statements) allow us to distinguish six firms' paths inside corporate financial distress (Table 2.2). On one hand, case 1 and case 2 regard firms facing a condition of *temporary financial distress*. While the first identifies a path of recovery to a viable financial situation that is fully disclosed in financial statements, the second represents a path of undetected fraud with recovery to a viable financial situation. On the other hand, case 3 and case 4 regard failing paths characterized by *severe financial distress* that can be either truly and fairly represented since its beginning (in case 3) or disclosed only after a fraud period (in case 4). There are two more final cases of corporate financial distress which have not been considered much in the academic debate because they are difficult to verify empirically. Such a lack can also be related to the absence of one or more conditions characterizing the "fraud triangle"[3] (Cressey 1953; Free and Murphy 2015). Case 5 corresponds to disclosed fraud after a temporary financial distress. Corporate fraud is usually disclosed after being perpetrated for a relatively long period of severe financial

---

[3] Cressey's (1953) fraud risk theory is based on three conditions (opportunity, pressure, and rationalization) that are always present in fraudulent actions: absent or ineffective controls; perceived financial need or pressure providing motivation to commit fraud; the fraudster's ability to rationalize that the fraudulent act is justified and consistent in some way with his or her values.

distress that implies especially bad financial consequences. It can be difficult to discover if perpetrated for short periods because there is not enough time to identify its signals. Such cases can be related to the so-called sudden bankruptcies (Hill et al. 1996) and "accidental bankruptcy" (Davis and Huang 2004). Finally, case 6 represents a situation of undetected fraud in spite of a long period of severe financial distress. Fraud is assumed to remain undetected only when corporate financial distress is temporary. The present book aims to consider also these last two cases in order to put the case for future research, given a lack of academic contributions and empirical evidence about them.

Summarizing, this paragraph provides a definition of financial distress as a path that may characterize corporate life. It may imply both the possibility and ultimately the event of bankruptcy. The time variable is essential in the analysis of such a path. Companies may recover after temporary financial distress. Failure follows a lasting condition of severe financial distress and has a negative epilogue called macro-failure that represents an important type of discontinuance in the corporate life cycle (Agostini 2013). So, both corporate failure and financial distress are extended in time (unlike bankruptcy), but they have different possible outcomes. Such differentiation permits us to identify a first criterion for categorizing corporate financial distress: the type of financial distress (either temporary or severe). A second criterion regards the presentation in financial statements of the consequences of corporate financial distress that may be (truly and fairly) represented in financial statements or hidden through fraud. According to the two criteria, six corporate paths are identified. Two of them (i.e. case 5 that corresponds to disclosed fraud after a temporary financial distress and case 6 that corresponds to undetected fraud in spite of a long period of severe financial distress) are especially worth considering because there appears to be a lack of academic contributions and empirical evidence about them.

2.3   PREVENTION AND EXPLANATION OF CORPORATE FINANCIAL DISTRESS

The concepts introduced in the previous paragraphs concerning corporate financial distress and failure are also relevant for understanding the passage of the focus in the academic debate from prediction to explanation. These are both relevant (in different ways, as explained below) for the evaluation and prevention of companies' financial deterioration. This paragraph is going to explore both prediction and explanation of corporate financial distress separately; then the move from one to the other will be analysed in order to identify reasons, differences, and benefits.

Since the earliest studies about *prediction*, financial distress has been considered a feature of corporate failure which in turn has been identified as an event characterizing the end of a firm's life cycle. This narrow definition has permitted the development of precise (and quite simple) statistical methods for financial distress prediction starting from the study by FitzPatrick (1932). Various modelling techniques have since been introduced throughout the world to predict the risk of business failure and to classify firms according to their financial health. Progressively, they have been based on different assumptions and specific computational complexities (Balcaen and Ooghe 2006). The most popular methods are still considered the cross-sectional statistical methods, which have resulted in numerous "single-period" static failure prediction models. Among them, univariate discriminant analysis (hereafter called UDA) and multiple discriminant analysis (hereafter called MDA) must be distinguished. Beaver (1966) develops the first (i.e. UDA), using a set of financial ratios and selecting them through a dichotomous classification test. Further developments of UDA (Tamari 1966; Moses and Liao 1987) use risk index models to predict failure: these models are simple and intuitive point systems, which are based on different ratios. Altman (1968) introduces the second (i.e. MDA) that is based on the estimation of a Z-score for predicting company failure. MDA is "a statistical technique used to classify an observation into one of several a priori groups dependent upon the observation's individual characteristics. It attempts to derive a linear (or quadratic) combination of these characteristics which best discriminates between the groups" (Altman 1968, p. 592). Over the years, there have been an enormous number of studies based on Altman's Z-score model. Altman et al. (1977) adjusted the original Z-score model into a different Zeta analysis model. Until the 1980s, the MDA technique dominated the literature on business failure prediction. These methods and contributions are valuable as milestones and are still the most used in failure prediction. They have been modified and applied in a variety of different ways (Taffler 1982) taking into consideration industrial enterprises (Deakin 1972, 1977; Blum 1974; Altman et al. 1977; Ohlson 1980), small firms (Edmister 1972), banks (Sinkey 1979), insurance companies (Trieschmann and Pinches 1973), stockbrokers (Altman and Loris 1976), building societies (Altman 1977), and railroads (Altman 1973). Moreover, they bring benefits for different users (e.g. creditors concerned with defaults, suppliers focused on repayment, and potential investors) and in a variety of applications, such as portfolio selection (Platt and Platt 1991), credit evaluation (Altman and Haldeman 1995), and turnaround management (Platt and Platt 1999). Beaver's UDA (1966), Altman's (1968) Z-score based on MDA, and their further developments represent, then, tools for differentiating between failed and non-failed firms. Since the introduction of these first predictive models, researchers have increasingly begun to take into account the *time variable* (Laitinen 1991; Ooghe and De Prijcker 2008; Balcaen and Ooghe 2006). This requires the application of more sophisticated methods for financial distress prediction, such as the use of neural networks (Fletcher and Goss 1993; Altman et al. 1994; Leshno and Spector 1996; Yang et al. 1999). These are based on artificial intelligence systems, which can be defined as computer programmes "that simulate the processes by which human learning and intuition take place" (Hawley et al. 1990). One example is the completion of expert systems with inductive learning algorithms. These methods are an attempt to derive rules by analysing a number of representative examples. Messier and Hansen (1988) are among the first to use this methodology in predicting loan default and bankruptcy. Odom and Sharda (1990) applied a neural network model to the case of bankruptcy prediction and compared it to classical discriminant analysis. Their results indicated that the classification ability of the neural network approach outperformed the classical techniques. Since then, numerous academic contributions have championed the study of corporate failure through a neural network approach. Though some of these have suggested that neural network models do not outperform statistical ones (Boritz and Kennedy 1995; Etheridge and Sriram 1997), most maintain that neural network models do offer a superior prediction accuracy to other statistical methods (Fletcher and Goss 1993; Leshno and Spector 1996; Pendharkar 2005; Yang et al. 1999; Zhang et al. 1999). Besides neural network, other artificial intelligence systems have also been applied in failure prediction (Sun and Li 2011). Some examples are decision tree (Frydman et al. 1985), genetic algorithm, rough sets, and case-based reasoning. All these methodologies have a role to play in forecasting financial distress, but they display a common drawback: they all focus on *static modelling for prediction*, being constructed only with sample data covering a certain period of time (Sun and Li 2011). They can, therefore, be properly applied to the prediction of bankruptcy, but that is only one of a large range of possible macro-failures characterizing the end corporate paths inside financial distress. This fact has long been ignored by prediction models. An arbitrary definition of failure may have serious consequences for the resulting failure prediction model (Balcaen and Ooghe 2006). Moreover, only the consideration of corporate financial distress (instead of the prediction of final bankruptcy) implies early warning of pathological situations and delivers notable benefits to a number of parties with an interest in the firm. For instance, management, shareholders, lenders, and auditors may gain the needed time to take action to reduce the costs which will be incurred if the firm fails without timely warning.

Recent predictive models aim to be more indicators of financial distress than predictors of bankruptcy. Much of prior research focuses on bankrupt versus stable firms, but, as Jones suggests, "accuracy in predicting bankruptcy among marginal companies, rather than quite healthy and quite distressed companies, may be the real test of a model's usefulness" (Jones 1987, p. 147). Recent research specifically identifies and documents the importance of examining financially distressed firms through prediction models that have evolved over time. The oldest models distinguish between financially distressed firms that survive and financially distressed firms that ultimately go bankrupt in order to offer incremental information to that learned from modelling stable firms and bankrupt firms. In fact, Gilbert et al. (1990) find different statistically significant explanatory financial variables to distinguish two groups of firms: financially distressed versus bankrupt, and stable versus bankrupt. Hopwood et al. (1994) also examine stressed and non-stressed firms, including in each group firms declared bankrupt. They also report that statistically significant variables differ between the two groups. More recent studies focus on reassessing the oldest models to determine whether they remain useful for predicting bankruptcy in more recent and longer periods and, more importantly, for predicting other financial distress conditions besides bankruptcy (Begley et al. 1996; Grice and Dugan 2001; Grice and Ingram 2001). The analysis of corporate financial distress is based on all currently available information relating to the company in order to evaluate if it will fall into the condition of default or financial difficulty (Zhou et al. 2015). For this reason, the traditional models described have been adapted so as to *predict corporate financial distress* instead of final (possible) bankruptcy. Three predictive models have proved to be adaptable and the most used in this sense (Pindado et al. 2008): the linear discriminant analysis introduced by Altman (1968), logistic analysis applied as an estimation method by Ohlson (1980), and the probit analysis implemented by Zmijewski

(1984). Grice and Dugan (2001) and Grice and Ingram (2001) provide empirical evidence in favour of the adaptation of these three predictive models as being still useful for predicting financial distress, but they indicate that the models' accuracy is significantly lower in recent periods. Results tend to improve when the models are re-estimated, but the magnitude and significance of the re-estimated coefficients differ from those reported in their original application. This suggests that there is no stable pattern in the coefficients of the seminal modes when applied to more recent and longer periods (Pindado et al. 2008). Thereafter, progressively other more complex statistical and data mining methods have been adapted to predict corporate financial distress, such as neural networks (Zhou et al. 2015; Wilson and Sharda 1994), decision trees (Gepp et al. 2010), and support vector machines (Shin et al. 2005). Fuzzy theory has been also applied in corporate financial distress prediction models (Ko et al. 2013; Chen et al. 2011). In addition, most recent research has developed hybrid models that are a combination of two or more methods (Divsalar et al. 2011; Verikas et al. 2010; Cho et al. 2010). The empirical results obtained by such hybrid models outperform those of single models, but they still present significant drawbacks.

Three main *drawbacks* concerning the described models for the prediction of corporate financial distress are reviewed here. First, the most evolved (recent) models, which provide the most accurate empirical results at the moment, are based on theories and modes of combining other (previous) methods that are not easy to explain clearly: this hinders to some degree their wide application in practice (Zhou et al. 2015). Second, the computations required by the most evolved models consume a lot of effort and time, impeding a widespread application. Even so, they are potentially interesting for users with the appropriate expertise and for certain objectives (e.g. researchers in their studies, creditors concerned with defaults, analysts and professional consultants, suppliers focused on repayments, potential investors). For this reason, the most used models for the prediction of corporate financial distress display a balanced combination of easy statistical application and accuracy of results. This reduces training costs and waste of time. Third, the passage of time prevents such static models from effectively forecasting financial distress in the changing economic environment or the changing enterprise operational environment. In the changing real world, new financially distressed enterprises gradually emerge to provide sample data flow (Sun and Li 2011). For this reason, predictive models are constructed only with sample data from a certain period of time. The introduction of evolved methods requires a considerable range of samples and fine-tuning, but these cannot then be applied consistently and constantly because they do not take into full account the changing economic environment over time (Sun et al. 2016). This implies the need to continuously monitor the performance of such predictive models for them to be truly predictive in a statistical sense. These doubts related to the described drawbacks can be aptly summarized in the questions put in an academic paper some years ago that are still valid for evaluating the usefulness of the current predictive models: "Are the statistical models capturing the dimensions of financial health which are important to the decision context? Do they work better than other techniques? Do they work consistently over time? Can the models be improved upon?" (Keasey and Watson 1991, p. 90).

A further drawback about the predictive models we have been examining is that they do not take into consideration another relevant feature explored in the previous paragraph about corporate financial distress and failure: their representation in financial statements. Indeed, the information the model draws from the annual accounts may not, in fact, reflect reality. In particular, Van De Velde (1987) classifies two factors that might be responsible for firms' misclassification. In a first type of error, the annual account does not present a fair and true view of the firm's financial situation. In a second type of error, the model is ill-adapted to evaluating certain important factors concerning the situation of the firm because not all relevant information is considered by or incorporated in the model. Van De Velde also reports some regional differences in the discovered reasons for misclassification and emphasizes that the representativeness of the examined documents (i.e. the reflection of the fair and true view of the firm's situation) is inadequate in most cases. This especially happens in firms that are practising fraud and accounts manipulation. Thus the appropriateness of the predictive methods is also crucially dependent upon the assumptions made regarding the costs of misclassification and the structure and availability of the data. Models for predicting corporate financial distress should therefore be considered according to *two alternative uses*. The first concerns the monitoring of current corporate status by different interested parties: this is an ex ante approach that requires a trade-off between difficulty of application and accuracy of results in order to reduce professional training costs and time. The specific type of model will be chosen according to the type of firm, user, and purpose of application. In this way, predictive models are used in an operational context as a means for identifying firms that might experience financial distress in order to decide when to implement further detailed investigation. For instance, credit rating agencies just use their experience and judgement to select the relevant information for evaluating the credit risk of a particular company or individual with a simple scorecard instead of complex statistical models (Mays 2004). They use and select from the available information. The information related to a distressed company is huge, including macroeconomic situation, company characteristics, financial status, and market information. The procedure of selecting corporate features for financial distress prediction models is itself a matter of investigation in accounting and finance academic research (Zhou et al. 2015). Such models aim to provide a warning sign of a potential failure situation since the financial characteristics of the firm under investigation resemble those of firms which have previously gone bankrupt more than those which are a priori healthy. Such an approach would still appear predictive in a statistical sense in that the probability of a firm classified as at risk actually failing is very significantly higher than that for a firm selected at random, and that of a firm not so classified is very significantly lower. According to this first (operational) use, predictive models are intended to be practical instruments mainly for external analysts. For this reason, they focus on visible consequences of financial distress and they are framed to make use of mainly quantitative annual account data as input for the instrument (i.e. information that the external analyst can collect more or less easily). The second alternative use of such methods aims to distinguish on an ex post basis between distressed firms. It is essentially descriptive in nature and emphasizes firms' features in a multivariate context. In this case, the predictive models do not aim to be universally applied because they focus on events characterizing different firms and time periods. They take into account the institutional and regulatory framework within which firms operate, and take into consideration the fact that legal regulations are subject to changes which radically alter the type, incidence, and costs associated with particular forms of financial distress. *The temporal perspective* (either ex ante or ex post) is what differentiates the two alternative uses of predictive models of corporate financial distress. Indeed, the importance of time gives such models a new usefulness in attempting to overcome the recognized limit of subsequent intertemporal validity due to natural changes in the general environment around the company. The prediction accuracy necessitates a consideration of time. This is especially evident in the light of life cycle theory, introduced in paragraph 2.1., which requires a consideration of the concept drift. This is due to the passage of time and the dynamic evolution of an enterprise: the consequences of financial distress experienced by a concrete enterprise will change as it evolves from one stage of its life cycle to another (Sun and Li 2011). Corporate financial distress generally implies deficiency of liquidity or cash flow difficulty in the starting-up period, excessive risk of financial leverage in the growing period, substantial or consecutive reduction in profitability in the maturing period, insolvency or bankruptcy in the recession period. The listed general consequences of corporate financial distress according to the temporal evolution of firms would require the recalibrating or substitution of prediction models every time the analysed firm moves from one stage to the other because of the financial distress concept drift (Sun and Li 2011). This phenomenon implies high costs, waste of time, difficultly (and possible errors) of application, inaccuracy of results, and so on. It seems preferable to consider the application of predictive models according to the second use described above as a premise for a deeper explanation of corporate financial distress. These considerations illustrate the reasons of the *progressive move from mere prediction to a fuller explanation of corporate financial distress* (Tinoco and Wilson 2013; Givoly et al. 2017) in order to examine closely how companies mutate from surviving (or even successful) into distressed and possibly bankrupt ones (Cybinski 2001; Parker 2012). Traditionally, prediction and explanation have been kept separate in default academic literature. For practical and commercial reasons, predictive models which estimate risk of failure and/or give a warning of imminent bankruptcy have been the "holy grail" of researchers. Such models are based on sophisticated techniques for discriminating failed from prosperous firms (often with an ex post view) producing precise results, but with a limited area of applicability (Cybinski 2001). While the prediction of corporate financial distress is relevant prevalently for external stakeholders, its explanation implies a deep analysis of corporate trajectories and is also relevant for internal parties, not least in order to avoid the same mistakes in the future. Indeed, while the prediction of corporate financial distress focuses on past and present time, the explanation considers all time dimensions (including the future). Moreover, while the prediction of corporate financial distress assumes a negative meaning (it aims at anticipating a pathological situation that firms are not prone to disclose), its explanation does not (it aims at understanding causes and consequences of a corporate status to avoid making the same mistakes in the future). Newer studies focus on understanding corporate failure: its theoretical exploration is today considered the essential premise for its prediction even though with a greater complexity and a consequent lower reliability of the models. Such understanding is based on a distress continuum to detect signals of a firm's deteriorating condition over time. Corporate paths, such as financial distress and failure, should be investigated because (negative) situations lasting over time are related to several factors. The explanation of such corporate paths requires the analysis of their causes (also non-financial factors) as financial distress is so called because its symptoms (or consequences) are financial, but its causes may also be related to non-financial factors. Such an explanation does not only focus on financial ratios and accounting items: it also considers other measures and events.

Summarizing, this paragraph has focused on the progressive move of academic literature from mere prediction to a fuller explanation of corporate financial distress. Concerning the first, the oldest predictive methods distinguish surviving from bankrupt companies. Their subsequent adjustments have aimed to predict corporate failure and, finally, the preceding financial distress. Such developments imply an increase in sophistication level, effort, time, and training costs of implementation. Moreover, prediction models cannot be indiscriminately applied: their intertemporal validity needs to be controlled, especially because of concept drift. These drawbacks explain why predictive models may be useful in two ways. First, they are used in a specific operational context (e.g. by credit rating agencies) to identify *ex ante* the corporate cases that need further detailed investigation. Second, they are used to distinguish on an *ex post* basis between distressed firms and to emphasize their features in multivariate contexts. The two uses assume a different temporal perspective, but both represent a premise for further explanation of corporate financial distress. This considers corporate events, and is especially based on the analysis of managers' strategies implemented to reduce firms' distress and affecting the likelihood of recovery (Koh et al. 2015), while also examining auditors' work before the issuance of qualified opinions.

2.4   Who Evaluates Corporate Financial Distress?

The analysis of corporate financial distress is very important for several parties, such as investors, company's partners, lending institutions, management, employees or their unions, auditors, credit insurers, suppliers, or retailers (Zhou et al. 2015), but also government regulators, and other stakeholders. The (different) interests of so many parties have driven a lot of studies on the issue of corporate financial distress. Its consideration implies early warning of pathological situations and confers large benefits to these various parties who have an interest in the firm and may be able to take action to reduce the costs which would be incurred if the firm fails without advance warning. This potential benefit explains the ongoing research in this area that continues to refine financial distress models as emphasized in the previous paragraph. All the interested parties are especially afraid of the (costly) financial consequences of corporate financial distress for the reasons described above: distressed firms have a tendency to do things that are harmful to debt holders, shareholders, and non-financial stakeholders (i.e. customers, suppliers, and employees), impairing access to credit and raising the cost of stakeholder relationships (Opler and Titman 1994). These tendencies are due to conflicts of interest between borrowers and lenders (Jensen and Meckling 1976; Myers 1977; Stulz 1990), between firms and their non-financial stakeholders (Baxter 1967; Titman 1984; Maksimovic and Titman 1991), and between shareholders and managers (Gilson and Vetsuypens 1993; Novaes and Zingales 1993). Moreover, distressed firms have lower-quality ERM programmes because of resource constraints inhibiting the investment necessary for effective ERM (Baxter et al. 2013). During corporate financial distress, ERM is especially relevant because it has been shown to be associated with better corporate governance (i.e. audit committees charged with direct oversight of risk), less audit-related risk (i.e. stable auditor relationships and effective internal controls), the presence of risk committees, and boards with longer tenure.

Many parties, then, with different interests are involved in a firm's financially distressed status, but they may be broadly differentiated: external and internal stakeholders have different possible available approaches to analysing corporate status. As emphasized in the previous paragraph, an ex ante approach can be only predictive for *external parties* seeking to capture relevant warnings of corporate financial distress in time. Indeed, parties external to the firm, such as investors, creditors, auditors, government regulators, and other stakeholders, have traditionally tried to assess the financial strength of companies (Platt and Platt 2002). In particular, investors and credit lenders need to evaluate the status of financial distress before they make any investment or credit granting decisions on the company, in order to avoid suffering losses. The same considerations are valid for stockholders that aim to avoid both direct costs (legal and administrative costs of restructuring the firm's debt) and indirect ones (the opportunity loss suffered when corporate resources are diverted to the debt restructuring process from more productive uses).

The explanation of corporate financial distress requires deep involvement and the availability of proper information. *Suppliers and customers*, differently from the other external parties recalled above, may gather relevant information and distress signals such as delayed shipments, problems with product quality, warnings from the supplier's bank, or observations made during company visits indicating near-term financial difficulties. From a supply chain management perspective, manufacturers are concerned about the financial health of their suppliers and vice versa (Platt and Platt 2002). A company's suppliers or retailers conduct credit transactions with the company and they therefore need to fully understand the company's financial status and make decisions about such transactions. Especially when there are long-term contracts with selected suppliers, large manufacturers seek out relevant information and are increasingly interested in the financial health of such suppliers in order to avoid disruption to their own production and distribution schedules. It is in both parties' interest to identify and reduce corporate financial distress. In this case, prediction and explanation of such negative status may be profitably combined. This is possible only for some stakeholders, especially managers and auditors.

The evaluation of corporate financial distress is based on knowledge of relevant conditions and events. It can be implemented, in the first instance, by managers and auditors (through the auditing procedures performed during a financial statement audit). From the beginning, default literature has emphasized the "stigma" of default that causes considerable damage to managers' reputations (Stein 1989). This explains *managers'* tendency to reduce the level of corporate financial distress by borrowing less, choosing less risky investment projects, and managing their firms more efficiently. A distinction may be introduced: in the presence of temporary financial distress, managers will rationally favour investment and financing policies that reduce the probability of financial distress (Gilson 1989), but when the negative situation becomes severer other less rational decisions may be considered. This is also related to the negative association between the level of corporate financial distress and the quality of ERM described above. Moreover, several types of corporate policy decisions seem likely to be influenced by the personal costs that managers incur because of such distress. There is empirical evidence about the turnover of senior managers in financially distressed firms: there is an increasing changeover in the group of individuals who between them hold the titles of CEO, president, and chairman of the board when firms experience financial distress. Auditing research has also noted that auditors' resignations are related to the increase of business risk. Indeed, it suggests three ways of working that appear to be the most used by *auditors* when firms experience financial distress. First, auditors may adjust the audit plan and increase audit fees, fearing an increased possibility of violations committed by a distressed firm (Menon and Williams 2001; Pratt and Stice 1994; Bell et al. 2001; Hay et al. 2006). Second, withdrawing their services confirms auditors' independence from a distressed firm, reducing the risks of both litigation and loss (Krishnan and Krishnan 1996; Simunic and Stein 1990; Bockus and Gigler 1998; Shu 2000). Third, auditors may modify their assessments and issue a going concern opinion in case of corporate financial distress (especially when it is severe). Concerning this third reaction, auditing research analyses the biunivocal relationship between corporate financial distress and auditors' evaluation: financially distressed firms are more likely to receive a qualified audit report (Citron and Taffler 1992; Hudaib and Cooke 2005; Geiger et al. 2005; Mutchler 1985; Chen and Church 1992; Krishnan and Krishnan 1996) and such qualified audit opinion signals that a firm is experiencing financial distress (Cybinski 2001). For this reason, going concern opinions reduce the unexpectedness of firms' Chap. 11 (bankruptcy) filing (Chen and Church 1992). The formation of an auditor's going concern opinion consists of two stages (Krishnan and Krishnan 1996; Asare et al. 2012). In the first stage, auditors form an initial impression of a firm's financial condition based on the available information. This first stage depends on the auditor's competence: even though most auditing research shows that auditors have the ability to identify a distressed company with going concern problems, there is empirical evidence that many companies in the year prior to bankruptcy receive an unqualified audit report without signals of going concern uncertainty (Behn et al. 1997; Citron and Taffler 1992; Lennox 1999; Menon and Schwartz 1987). This is connected to the second stage, where auditors decide the type of audit report to be issued, which is itself related to auditors' independence: acting as rational economic agents, auditors are influenced by the perceived consequences of issuing a going concern report (DeAngelo 1981; Watts and Zimmerman 1983). Risk of litigation, risk of loss of reputation, and risk of client loss (Mutchler 1985) are factors suggested in the literature as related to the economic trade-offs faced by the auditors (Krishnan and Krishnan 1996), influencing their going concern opinion and final decision. The risk of litigation and risk of loss of reputation may have a positive effect on auditor independence, while the risk of audit loss may compromise auditor independence. The competence and independence of audit firms are also influenced by their sizes. Large audit firms are more likely to issue a qualified audit opinion than smaller ones (Warren 1980). Moreover, they are better funded and more likely to disclose problems because of their greater risk exposure (Dye 1993). Consequently, due to their fear of financial problems being disclosed, financially distressed firms are less likely to use one of the "Big Four" audit firms[4] (Miglani et al. 2015). Major streams of literature recognize that the main causes of audit failures lie in the audit expectation gap (Porter 1993; Salehi 2011) and in the lack of auditors' independence. For this reason, auditor rotation literature (Stefaniak et al. 2009) suggests setting a limit on auditor tenure in order to increase auditor independence and improve objectivity: auditors are less likely to form relationships with their clients if they have a shorter tenure. Thus, on the one hand, limited auditor tenure improves audit quality; on the other mandatory rotation increases audit costs and wastes the knowledge that the auditor has accumulated over time. In the same way, the choice between external or internal auditing implies a trade-off between auditors' competency and objectivity (Kofman and Lawarree 1993): internal auditors have more information about the operations of their firm and can produce higher-quality reports, but they are also more prone to collusion with the management. Moreover, assuming that internal auditors rarely change their auditing methods, whereas different external audit firms use different audit technologies, rotation makes external auditing more effective than internal auditing in preventing fraud. In both cases (i.e. internal and external), auditors can limit fraudsters' "learning their tricks" by randomizing their strategy over different audit technologies and using different individual auditors. When a fraudster is allowed to face the same audit technology many times, he or she can explore its loopholes and use that information to cheat, so the efficacy of an audit technology diminishes over time. In the same way, companies audited by the same firm over time may also learn how to

---

[4] The "Big Four" audit firms are KPMG, Deloitte Touche Tohmatsu, Pricewaterhouse Coopers, and Ernst & Young.

manipulate their financial statements without being caught. Rotating audit firms reduces such opportunities.

This may represent an effective audit strategy in a principal–agent framework, in order to avoid the undesired action of an agent (i.e. a distressed firm) successfully passing an audit. According to the same agency theory, auditors can also become the agent because of information asymmetry: agents (auditors in this case) enjoy a competitive advantage over principals (external stakeholders of a distressed firm) because of the "privileged" information they have about the company. Information within an organization is critical, and auditors working with the management of a company are likely to be aware of essential information. On the one hand, such collaboration is positive: auditors' work supplements managers' evaluations based on the up-to-date and relevant information at their disposal. This is consistent with belief-revision research in auditing (Asare 1992; Bhaskar et al. 2017). On the other hand, there is always the possibility of collusion between auditors and managers (Olsen and Torsvik 1998; Tirole 1986). Information asymmetry can be used in illegal or legal but unethical ways to maximize agents' interests at the expense of the principals. This results in the principals' inability to control what they might reasonably expect to be the actions of the agent (Strausz 1997).

In summary, while the previous paragraph emphasized the relevance of both prediction and explanation of corporate financial distress for different parties, this paragraph distinguishes stakeholders according to the relevance of information at their disposal for evaluating corporate financial distress. After considering the distress signals that can be gathered from suppliers and customers, the paragraph focuses on managers' evaluation and auditors' opinion. With regard to the first, managers' actions to reduce corporate financial distress may be different according to its type (either temporary or severe). This is also related to ERM and management turnover. Regarding the second, academic contributions focus on three auditors' reactions (i.e. adjusting the audit plan and increasing audit fees, withdrawing from their engagement, issuing a modified going concern opinion) and three types of risks (i.e. risk of litigation, risk of loss of reputation and risk of client loss) in order to evaluate auditors' competence and independence when audited firms are experiencing financial distress. Moreover, the doubled evaluations of managers and auditors may either be positive or increase the risk of collusion. The next chapter will investigate such evaluations in the US context.

BIBLIOGRAPHY

Acharya, V. V., Bharath, S. T., & Srinivasan, A. (2007). Does industry-wide distress affect defaulted firms? Evidence from creditor recoveries. *Journal of Financial Economics, 85*(3), 787–821.

Agostini, M. (2013). Two common steps in firms' failing path. *Risk Governance & Control: Financial Markets & Institutions, 3*(1), 115–128.

Altman, E. I. (1968). Financial ratios, discriminant analysis and the prediction of corporate bankruptcy. *The Journal of Finance, 23*(4), 589–609.

Altman, E. I. (1973). Predicting railroad bankruptcies in America. *The Bell Journal of Economics and Management Science, 4*, 184–211.

Altman, E. I. (1977). Predicting performance in the savings and loan association industry. *Journal of Monetary Economics, 3*(4), 443–466.

Altman, E. I. (1984). A further empirical investigation of the bankruptcy cost question. *The Journal of Finance, 39*(4), 1067–1089.

Altman, E. I. (1993). Evaluating the chapter 11 bankruptcy-reorganization process. *Columbia Business Law Review, 1*.

Altman, E. I., & Eisenbeis, R. A. (1978). Financial applications of discriminant analysis: A clarification. *Journal of Financial and Quantitative Analysis, 13*(1), 185–195.

Altman, E. I., & Haldeman, R. G. (1995). Corporate credit-scoring models: Approaches and tests for successful implementation. *Journal of Commercial Lending, 77*(9), 10–22.

Altman, E. I., Haldeman, R. G., & Narayanan, P. (1977). ZETATM analysis a new model to identify bankruptcy risk of corporations. *Journal of Banking & Finance, 1*(1), 29–54.

Altman, E. I., & Hotchkiss, E. (2006). *Corporate financial distress and bankruptcy: Predict and avoid bankruptcy, analyze and invest in distressed debt*. Hoboken: Wiley Finance.

Altman, E. I., & Hotchkiss, E. (2010). *Corporate financial distress and bankruptcy: Predict and avoid bankruptcy, analyze and invest in distressed debt* (Vol. 289). Hoboken, NJ: John Wiley & Sons.

Altman, E. I., & Loris, B. (1976). A financial early warning system for over-the-counter broker-dealers. *The Journal of Finance, 31*(4), 1201–1217.

Altman, E. I., Marco, G., & Varetto, F. (1994). Corporate distress diagnosis: Comparisons using linear discriminant analysis and neural networks (the Italian experience). *Journal of Banking & Finance, 18*(3), 505–529.

Andrade, G., & Kaplan, S. N. (1998). How costly is financial (not economic) distress? Evidence from highly leveraged transactions that became distressed. *The Journal of Finance, 53*(5), 1443–1493.

Anthony, J. H., & Ramesh, K. (1992). Association between accounting performance measures and stock prices: A test of the life cycle hypothesis. *Journal of Accounting and Economics, 15*(2–3), 203–227.

Arens, A. A., Elder, R. J., & Beasley, M. S. (2003). *Auditing and assurance services, an integral approach.* New Delhi: Prentice Hall Publisher.

Argenti, J. (1976). Corporate planning and corporate collapse. *Long Range Planning, 9*(6), 12–17.

Asare, S. K. (1992). The auditor's going-concern decision: Interaction of task variables and the sequential processing of evidence. *Accounting Review, 67,* 379–393.

Asare, S. K., Fitzgerald, B. C., Graham, L. E., Joe, J. R., Negangard, E. M., & Wolfe, C. J. (2012). Auditors' internal control over financial reporting decisions: Analysis, synthesis, and research directions. *Auditing: A Journal of Practice & Theory, 32*(sp1), 131–166.

Asquith, P., Gertner, R., & Scharfstein, D. (1994). Anatomy of financial distress: An examination of junk-bond issuers. *The Quarterly Journal of Economics, 109*(3), 625–658.

Baer, M. H. (2008). Linkage and the deterrence of corporate fraud. *Virginia Law Review, 94,* 1295–1365.

Balcaen, S., Manigart, S., Buyze, J., & Ooghe, H. (2012). Firm exit after distress: Differentiating between bankruptcy, voluntary liquidation and M&A. *Small Business Economics, 39*(4), 949–975.

Balcaen, S., & Ooghe, H. (2006). 35 years of studies on business failure: An overview of the classic statistical methodologies and their related problems. *The British Accounting Review, 38*(1), 63–93.

Barker, V. L., III, & Duhaime, I. M. (1997). Strategic change in the turnaround process: Theory and empirical evidence. *Strategic Management Journal, 18,* 13–38.

Barnes, M. (Ed.). (1990). *Financial control.* London: Thomas Telford.

Barnes, P. (1987). The analysis and use of financial ratios: A review article. *Journal of Business Finance & Accounting, 14*(4), 449–461.

Baum, J. A., & Mezias, S. J. (1992). Localized competition and organizational failure in the Manhattan hotel industry, 1898–1990. *Administrative Science Quarterly, 37,* 580–604.

Baxter, N. D. (1967). Leverage, risk of ruin and the cost of capital. *The Journal of Finance, 22*(3), 395–403.

Baxter, R., Bedard, J. C., Hoitash, R., & Yezegel, A. (2013). Enterprise risk management program quality: Determinants, value relevance, and the financial crisis. *Contemporary Accounting Research, 30*(4), 1264–1295.

Beasley, M., Branson, B., & Hancock, B. (2015). *Report on the current state of enterprise risk oversight: Update on trends and opportunities.* Research conducted by the ERM Initiative at North Carolina State University on behalf of the American Institute of CPAs Business, Industry & Government Team, 12.

Beaver, W. H. (1966). Financial ratios as predictors of failure. *Journal of Accounting Research, 4,* 71–111.

Begley, J., Ming, J., & Watts, S. (1996). Bankruptcy classification errors in the 1980s: An empirical analysis of Altman's and Ohlson's models. *Review of Accounting Studies, 1*(4), 267–284.

Behn, B. K., Carcello, J. V., Hermanson, D. R., & Hermanson, R. H. (1997). The determinants of audit client satisfaction among clients of big 6 firms. *Accounting Horizons, 11*(1), 7–24.

Bell, T. B., Landsman, W. R., & Shackelford, D. A. (2001). Auditors' perceived business risk and audit fees: Analysis and evidence. *Journal of Accounting Research, 39*(1), 35–43.

Beynon, M. J., & Peel, M. J. (2001). Variable precision rough set theory and data discretisation: An application to corporate failure prediction. *Omega, 29*(6), 561–576.

Bhaskar, L. S., Krishnan, G. V., & Yu, W. (2017). Debt covenant violations, firm financial distress, and auditor actions. *Contemporary Accounting Research, 34*(1), 186–215.

Blocher, E., Ko, L. J., & Lin, P. (1999). Prediction of corporate financial distress: An application of the composite rule induction system. *The International Journal of Digital Accounting Research, 1*(1), 69–85.

Blum, M. (1974). Failing company discriminant analysis. *Journal of Accounting Research, 12*, 1–25.

Bockus, K., & Gigler, F. (1998). A theory of auditor resignation. *Journal of Accounting Research, 36*(2), 191–208.

Boritz, J. E., & Kennedy, D. B. (1995). Effectiveness of neural network types for prediction of business failure. *Expert Systems with Applications, 9*(4), 503–512.

Charan, R., Useem, J., & Harrington, A. (2002). Why companies fail CEOs offer every excuse but the right one: Their own errors. Here are ten mistakes to avoid. *Fortune-European Edition, 145*(11), 36–46.

Chen, H. L., Yang, B., Wang, G., Liu, J., Xu, X., Wang, S. J., et al. (2011). A novel bankruptcy prediction model based on an adaptive fuzzy k-nearest neighbor method. *Knowledge-Based Systems, 24*(8), 1348–1359.

Chen, K. C., & Church, B. K. (1992). Default on debt obligations and the issuance of going-concern opinions. *Auditing, 11*(2), 30.

Chen, Y., Weston, J. F., & Altman, E. I. (1995). Financial distress and restructuring models. *Financial Management, 24*, 57–75.

Cho, S., Hong, H., & Ha, B. C. (2010). A hybrid approach based on the combination of variable selection using decision trees and case-based reasoning using the Mahalanobis distance: For bankruptcy prediction. *Expert Systems with Applications, 37*(4), 3482–3488.

Citron, D. B., & Taffler, R. J. (1992). The audit report under going concern uncertainties: An empirical analysis. *Accounting and Business Research, 22*(88), 337–345.

Cohen, J., Krishnamoorthy, G., & Wright, A. (2017). Enterprise risk management and the financial reporting process: The experiences of audit committee members, CFOs, and external auditors. *Contemporary Accounting Research, 34*(2), 1178–1209.

Committee of Sponsoring Organizations of the Treadway Commission, The (COSO). (2004). *Enterprise Risk Management-Integrated Framework: Executive Summary.*

Covitz, D. M., Han, S., & Wilson, B. A. (2006). Are longer bankruptcies really more costly? *Finance and Economics Discussion Series 2006-27.* Washington: Board of Governors of the Federal Reserve System. Retrieved from SSRN: https://ssrn.com/abstract=891486 or Retrieved October 6, 2017, from https://doi.org/10.2139/ssrn.891486

Cressey, D. R. (1953). *Other people's money: A study of the social psychology of embezzlement.* New York: Free Press.

Cybinski, P. (2001). Description, explanation, prediction–the evolution of bankruptcy studies? *Managerial Finance, 27*(4), 29–44.

Daily, C. M., & Dalton, D. R. (1995). CEO and director turnover in failing firms: An illusion of change? *Strategic Management Journal, 16*(5), 393–400.

Davis, A. H., & Huang, X. (2004, October). The stock performance of firms emerging from Chapter 11 and accidental bankruptcy. In *FMA Meeting,* New Orleans, USA (pp. 6–9).

Deakin, E. B. (1972). A discriminant analysis of predictors of business failure. *Journal of Accounting Research, 10,* 167–179.

Deakin, E. B. (1977). Business failure prediction: An empirical analysis. In E. I. Altman & A. W. Sametz (Eds.), *Financial crises: Institutions and markets in a fragile environment. Chapter 4* (pp. 72–88). New York: John Wiley & Sons.

DeAngelo, L. E. (1981). Auditor size and audit quality. *Journal of Accounting and Economics, 3*(3), 183–199.

Denis, D. J., & Kruse, T. A. (2000). Managerial discipline and corporate restructuring following performance declines. *Journal of Financial Economics, 55*(3), 391–424.

Dimitras, A. I., Slowinski, R., Susmaga, R., & Zopounidis, C. (1999). Business failure prediction using rough sets. *European Journal of Operational Research, 114*(2), 263–280.

Divsalar, M., Javid, M. R., Gandomi, A. H., Soofi, J. B., & Mahmood, M. V. (2011). Hybrid genetic programming-based search algorithms for enterprise bankruptcy prediction. *Applied Artificial Intelligence, 25*(8), 669–692.

Donovan, J., Frankel, R. M., & Martin, X. (2015). Accounting conservatism and creditor recovery rate. *The Accounting Review, 90*(6), 2267–2303.

Dye, R. A. (1993). Auditing standards, legal liability, and auditor wealth. *Journal of Political Economy, 101*(5), 887–914.

Edmister, R. O. (1972). An empirical test of financial ratio analysis for small business failure prediction. *Journal of Financial and Quantitative Analysis, 7*(2), 1477–1493.

Edwards, A., Schwab, C., & Shevlin, T. (2013, February). Financial constraints and the incentive for tax planning. In *2013 American Taxation Association Midyear Meeting: New Faculty/Doctoral Student Session* (Vol. 2216875). Retrieved October 6, 2017, from http://papers.ssrn.com/abstract

Elloumi, F., & Gueyie, J. P. (2001). Financial distress and corporate governance: An empirical analysis. *Corporate Governance: The International Journal of Business in Society, 1*(1), 15–23.

Erickson, M., Heitzman, S., & Zhang, X. F. (2011). Accounting fraud and the market for corporate control. *University of Chicago, Booth School of Business Working Paper*. Retrieved October 6, 2017, from http://www.aaifm.org/Archive/Accounting%20Fraud.pdf

Etheridge, H. L., & Sriram, R. S. (1997). A comparison of the relative costs of financial distress models: Artificial neural networks, logit and multivariate discriminant analysis. *Intelligent Systems in Accounting, Finance and Management, 6*(3), 235–248.

Everett, J., & Watson, J. (1998). Small business failure and external risk factors. *Small Business Economics, 11*(4), 371–390.

Ferris, S. P., Jayaraman, N., & Makhija, A. K. (1997). The response of competitors to announcements of bankruptcy: An empirical examination of contagion and competitive effects. *Journal of Corporate Finance, 3*(4), 367–395.

FitzPatrick, P. J. (1932). A comparison of the ratios of successful industrial enterprises with those of failed companies. *Certified Public Accountant, 2*, 598–605.

Flagg, J. C., Giroux, G. A., & Wiggins, C. E. (1991). Predicting corporate bankruptcy using failing firms. *Review of Financial Economics, 1*(1), 67–78.

Fletcher, D., & Goss, E. (1993). Forecasting with neural networks: An application using bankruptcy data. *Information Management, 24*(3), 159–167.

Free, C., & Murphy, P. R. (2015). The ties that bind: The decision to co-offend in fraud. *Contemporary Accounting Research, 32*(1), 18–54.

Frydman, H., Altman, E. I., & Kao, D. L. (1985). Introducing recursive partitioning for financial classification: The case of financial distress. *The Journal of Finance, 40*(1), 269–291.

Geiger, M. A., Raghunandan, K., & Rama, D. V. (2005). Recent changes in the association between bankruptcies and prior audit opinions. *Auditing: A Journal of Practice & Theory, 24*(1), 21–35.

Gepp, A., Kumar, K., & Bhattacharya, S. (2010). Business failure prediction using decision trees. *Journal of Forecasting, 29*(6), 536–555.

Gilbert, L. R., Menon, K., & Schwartz, K. B. (1990). Predicting bankruptcy for firms in financial distress. *Journal of Business Finance & Accounting, 17*(1), 161–171.

Gilson, S. C. (1989). Management turnover and financial distress. *Journal of Financial Economics, 25*(2), 241–262.

Gilson, S. C., & Vetsuypens, M. R. (1993). CEO compensation in financially distressed firms: An empirical analysis. *The Journal of Finance, 48*(2), 425–458.

Givoly, D., Hayn, C., & Katz, S. (2017). The changing relevance of accounting information to debt holders over time. *Review of Accounting Studies, 22*(1), 64–108.

Greening, D. W., & Johnson, R. A. (1996). Do managers and strategies matter? A study in crisis. *Journal of Management Studies, 33*(1), 25–51.

Grice, J. S., & Dugan, M. T. (2001). The limitations of bankruptcy prediction models: Some cautions for the researcher. *Review of Quantitative Finance and Accounting, 17*(2), 151–166.

Grice, J. S., & Ingram, R. W. (2001). Tests of the generalizability of Altman's bankruptcy prediction model. *Journal of Business Research, 54*(1), 53–61.

Hambrick, D. C., & D'Aveni, R. A. (1992). Top team deterioration as part of the downward spiral of large corporate bankruptcies. *Management Science, 38*(10), 1445–1466.

Hasan, M. M., Hossain, M., & Habib, A. (2015). Corporate life cycle and cost of equity capital. *Journal of Contemporary Accounting and Economics, 11*(1), 46–60.

Hawley, D. D., Johnson, J. D., & Raina, D. (1990). Artificial neural systems: A new tool for financial decision-making. *Financial Analysts Journal, 46*(6), 63–72.

Hay, D. C., Knechel, W. R., & Wong, N. (2006). Audit fees: A meta-analysis of the effect of supply and demand attributes. *Contemporary Accounting Research, 23*(1), 141–191.

Hendel, I. (1996). Competition under financial distress. *The Journal of Industrial Economics, 44*, 309–324.

Hertzel, M. G., Li, Z., Officer, M. S., & Rodgers, K. J. (2008). Inter-firm linkages and the wealth effects of financial distress along the supply chain. *Journal of Financial Economics, 87*(2), 374–387.

Hertzel, M. G., & Smith, J. K. (1993). Industry effects of interfirm lawsuits: Evidence from Pennzoil v. Texaco. *Journal of Law, Economics, and Organization, 9*, 425.

Hill, N. T., Perry, S. E., & Andes, S. (1996). Evaluating firms in financial distress: An event history analysis. *Journal of Applied Business Research, 12*(3), 60.

Hopwood, W., McKeown, J. C., & Mutchler, J. F. (1994). A reexamination of auditor versus model accuracy within the context of the going-concern opinion decision. *Contemporary Accounting Research, 10*(2), 409–431.

Hoyt, R. E., & Liebenberg, A. P. (2011). The value of enterprise risk management. *The Journal of Risk and Insurance, 78*(4), 795–822.

Hudaib, M., & Cooke, T. E. (2005). The impact of managing director changes and financial distress on audit qualification and auditor switching. *Journal of Business Finance & Accounting, 32*(9–10), 1703–1739.

Jenkins, D. S., Kane, G. D., & Velury, U. (2004). The impact of the corporate life-cycle on the value-relevance of disaggregated earnings components. *Review of Accounting and Finance, 3*(4), 5–20.

Jensen, M. C. (1991). Corporate control and the politics of finance. *Journal of Applied Corporate Finance, 4*, 13–33.

Jensen, M. C., & Meckling, W. H. (1976). Theory of the firm: Managerial behavior, agency costs and ownership structure. *Journal of Financial Economics, 3*(4), 305–360.

John, K., Lang, L. H., & Netter, J. (1992). The voluntary restructuring of large firms in response to performance decline. *The Journal of Finance, 47*(3), 891–917.

Jones, F. L. (1987). Current techniques in bankruptcy prediction. *Journal of Accounting Literature, 6*(1), 131–164.

Jones, M. (Ed.). (2011). *Creative accounting, fraud and international accounting scandals.* Chichester: John Wiley & Sons.

Kang, J. K., & Stulz, R. M. (2000). Do banking shocks affect borrowing firm performance? An analysis of the Japanese experience. *The Journal of Business, 73*(1), 1–23.

Kaplan, R., & Mikes, A. (2013, October 16). Towards a contingency theory of enterprise risk management. *AAA 2014 Management Accounting Section (MAS) Meeting Paper.* Available at SSRN: https://ssrn.com/abstract=2311293 or https://doi.org/10.2139/ssrn.2311293

Keasey, K., Pindado, J., & Rodrigues, L. (2015). The determinants of the costs of financial distress in SMEs. *International Small Business Journal, 33*(8), 862–881.

Keasey, K., & Watson, R. (1991). Financial distress prediction models: A review of their usefulness. *British Journal of Management, 2*(2), 89–102.

Ko, Y. C., Fujita, H., & Tzeng, G. H. (2013). A fuzzy integral fusion approach in analyzing competitiveness patterns from WCY2010. *Knowledge-Based Systems, 49*, 1–9.

Kofman, F., & Lawarree, J. (1993). Collusion in hierarchical agency. *Econometrica: Journal of the Econometric Society, 61*, 629–656.

Koh, S., Durand, R. B., Dai, L., & Chang, M. (2015). Financial distress: Lifecycle and corporate restructuring. *Journal of Corporate Finance, 33*, 19–33.

Kolay, M., Lemmon, M., & Tashjian, E. (2016). Spreading the misery? Sources of bankruptcy spillover in the supply chain. *Journal of Financial and Quantitative Analysis, 51*(6), 1955–1990.

Krishnan, J., & Krishnan, J. (1996). The role of economic trade-offs in the audit opinion decision: An empirical analysis. *Journal of Accounting, Auditing & Finance, 11*(4), 565–586.

Laitinen, E. K. (1991). Financial ratios and different failure processes. *Journal of Business Finance & Accounting, 18*(5), 649–673.

Lang, L. H., & Stulz, R. (1992). Contagion and competitive intra-industry effects of bankruptcy announcements: An empirical analysis. *Journal of Financial Economics, 32*(1), 45–60.

Lau, A. H. L. (1987). A five-state financial distress prediction model. *Journal of Accounting Research, 25*, 127–138.

Lennox, C. S. (1999). Audit quality and auditor size: An evaluation of reputation and deep pockets hypotheses. *Journal of Business Finance & Accounting, 26*(7–8), 779–805.

Leshno, M., & Spector, Y. (1996). Neural network prediction analysis: The bankruptcy case. *Neurocomputing, 10*(2), 125–147.

Lian, Y. (2017). Financial distress and customer-supplier relationships. *Journal of Corporate Finance, 43*, 397–406.

Maksimovic, V., & Titman, S. (1991). Financial policy and reputation for product quality. *The Review of Financial Studies, 4*(1), 175–200.

Mays, F. E. (2004). *Credit scoring for risk managers: The handbook for lenders.* Ohio: Thomson/South-Western.

Mcleay, S., & Omar, A. (2000). The sensitivity of prediction models to the non-normality of bounded and unbounded financial ratios. *The British Accounting Review, 32*(2), 213–230.

Menon, K., & Schwartz, K. B. (1987). An empirical investigation of audit qualification decisions in the presence of going concern uncertainties. *Contemporary Accounting Research, 3*(2), 302–315.

Menon, K., & Williams, D. D. (2001). Long-term trends in audit fees. *Auditing: A Journal of Practice & Theory, 20*(1), 115–136.

Messier, W. F., Jr., & Hansen, J. V. (1988). Inducing rules for expert system development: An example using default and bankruptcy data. *Management Science, 34*(12), 1403–1415.

Miglani, S., Ahmed, K., & Henry, D. (2015). Voluntary corporate governance structure and financial distress: Evidence from Australia. *Journal of Contemporary Accounting and Economics, 11*(1), 18–30.

Miller, D., & Friesen, P. H. (1984). A longitudinal study of the corporate life cycle. *Management Science, 30*(10), 1161–1183.

Moses, D., & Liao, S. S. (1987). On developing models for failure prediction. *Journal of Commercial Bank Lending, 69*(7), 27–38.

Mueller, D. C. (1972). A life cycle theory of the firm. *The Journal of Industrial Economics, 20*, 199–219.

Mutchler, J. F. (1985). A multivariate analysis of the auditor's going-concern opinion decision. *Journal of Accounting Research, 23*, 668–682.

Myers, S. C. (1977). Determinants of corporate borrowing. *Journal of Financial Economics, 5*(2), 147–175.

Nahar Abdullah, S. (2006). Board structure and ownership in Malaysia: The case of distressed listed companies. *Corporate Governance: The International Journal of Business in Society, 6*(5), 582–594.

Novaes, W., & Zingales, L. (1993). Financial distress as a collapse of incentive schemes. *Unpublished manuscript.* University of Chicago. Retrieved October 6, 2017, from https://bibliotecadigital.fgv.br/dspace/handle/10438/12273

Odom, M. D., & Sharda, R. (1990, June). A neural network model for bank-ruptcy prediction. In *Neural Networks, 1990. 1990 IJCNN International Joint Conference on* (pp. 163–168). IEEE. Retrieved October 6, 2017, from http://ieeexplore.ieee.org/document/5726669/

Ohlson, J. A. (1980). Financial ratios and the probabilistic prediction of bank-ruptcy. *Journal of Accounting Research, 18,* 109–131.

Olsen, T. E., & Torsvik, G. (1998). Collusion and renegotiation in hierarchies: A case of beneficial corruption. *International Economic Review, 39,* 413–438.

Ooghe, H., & De Prijcker, S. (2008). Failure processes and causes of company bankruptcy: A typology. *Management Decision, 46*(2), 223–242.

Ooghe, H., & Joos, P. (1990). *Failure prediction, explanation of misclassifications and incorporation of other relevant variables: Result of empirical research in Belgium.* Working paper, Department of Corporate Finance, Ghent University (Belgium).

Ooghe, H., Joos, P., & De Bourdeaudhuij, C. (1995). Financial distress models in Belgium: The results of a decade of empirical research. *The International Journal of Accounting, 30,* 245–274.

Ooghe, H., & Verbaere, E. (1985). Predicting business failure on the basis of accounting data: The Belgian experience. *The International Journal of Accounting, 9*(2), 19–44.

Opler, T. C., & Titman, S. (1994). Financial distress and corporate performance. *The Journal of Finance, 49*(3), 1015–1040.

Parker, L. D. (2012). Qualitative management accounting research: Assessing deliverables and relevance. *Critical Perspectives on Accounting, 23*(1), 54–70.

Pastor, L., & Veronesi, P. (2003). *Stock prices and IPO waves* (No. w9858). National Bureau of Economic Research.

Peel, M. J. (1990). *The liquidation/merger alternative: Theory and evidence.* Aldershot, UK: Avebury.

Peel, M. J., & Wilson, N. (1989). The liquidation/merger alternative some results for the UK corporate sector. *Managerial and Decision Economics, 10*(3), 209–220.

Pendharkar, P. C. (2005). A threshold-varying artificial neural network approach for classification and its application to bankruptcy prediction problem. *Computers & Operations Research, 32*(10), 2561–2582.

Pindado, J., Rodrigues, L., & de la Torre, C. (2008). Estimating financial distress likelihood. *Journal of Business Research, 61*(9), 995–1003.

Platt, H. D., & Platt, M. B. (1991). A note on the use of industry-relative ratios in bankruptcy prediction. *Journal of Banking & Finance, 15*(6), 1183–1194.

Platt, H. D., & Platt, M. B. (1999). The effects of leverage, management disci-pline, and cyclicality on leveraged buyout failure. *The Journal of Alternative Investments, 1*(4), 28–42.

Platt, H. D., & Platt, M. B. (2002). Predicting corporate financial distress: Reflections on choice-based sample bias. *Journal of Economics and Finance, 26*(2), 184–199.

Pompe, P. P., & Bilderbeek, J. (2005). The prediction of bankruptcy of small-and medium-sized industrial firms. *Journal of Business Venturing, 20*(6), 847–868.

Porter, B. (1993). An empirical study of the audit expectation-performance gap. *Accounting and Business Research, 24*(93), 49–68.

Pratt, J., & Stice, J. D. (1994). The effects of client characteristics on auditor litigation risk judgments, required audit evidence, and recommended audit fees. *Accounting Review, 69*, 639–656.

Salehi, M. (2011). Audit expectation gap: Concept, nature and trace. *African Journal of Business Management, 5*(21), 8376–8392.

Sanz, L. J., & Ayca, J. (2006). Financial distress costs in Latin America: A case study. *Journal of Business Research, 59*(3), 394–395.

Shin, K. S., Lee, T. S., & Kim, H. J. (2005). An application of support vector machines in bankruptcy prediction model. *Expert Systems with Applications, 28*(1), 127–135.

Shu, S. Z. (2000). Auditor resignations: Clientele effects and legal liability. *Journal of Accounting and Economics, 29*(2), 173–205.

Simunic, D. A., & Stein, M. T. (1990). Audit risk in a client portfolio context. *Contemporary Accounting Research, 6*(2), 329–343.

Sinkey, J. F. (1979). *Problem and failed institutions in the commercial banking industry* (pp. 34–39). Greenwich, CT: JAI Press.

Slovin, M. B., Sushka, M. E., & Polonchek, J. A. (1999). An analysis of contagion and competitive effects at commercial banks. *Journal of Financial Economics, 54*(2), 197–225.

Spence, A. M. (1977). Entry, capacity, investment and oligopolistic pricing. *The Bell Journal of Economics, 8*, 534–544.

Spence, A. M. (1979). Investment strategy and growth in a new market. *Journal of Reprints for Antitrust Law and Economics, 10*, 345.

Spence, A. M. (1981). The learning curve and competition. *The Bell Journal of Economics, 12*, 49–70.

Stefaniak, C. M., Robertson, J. C., & Houston, R. W. (2009). The causes and consequences of auditor switching: A review of the literature. *Journal of Accounting Literature, 28*, 47.

Stein, S. (1989). *A feast for lawyers: Inside chapter 11—An exposé.* New York: M Evans & Co.

Strausz, R. (1997). Delegation of monitoring in a principal-agent relationship. *The Review of Economic Studies, 64*(3), 337–357.

Stulz, R. (1990). Managerial discretion and optimal financing policies. *Journal of Financial Economics, 26*(1), 3–27.

Sudarsanam, S., & Lai, J. (2001). Corporate financial distress and turnaround strategies: An empirical analysis. *British Journal of Management, 12*(3), 183–199.

Sun, J., & Li, H. (2011). Dynamic financial distress prediction using instance selection for the disposal of concept drift. *Expert Systems with Applications, 38*(3), 2566–2576.

Sun, J., Li, H., Chang, P. C., & He, K. Y. (2016). The dynamic financial distress prediction method of EBW-VSTW-SVM. *Enterprise Information Systems, 10*(6), 611–638.

Sutton, R. I., & Callahan, A. L. (1987). The stigma of bankruptcy: Spoiled organizational image and its management. *Academy of Management Journal, 30*(3), 405–436.

Swaminathan, A. (1996). Environmental conditions at founding and organizational mortality: A trial-by-fire model. *Academy of Management Journal, 39*(5), 1350–1377.

Taffler, R. J. (1982). Forecasting company failure in the UK using discriminant analysis and financial ratio data. *Journal of the Royal Statistical Society. Series A (General), 145*, 342–358.

Tamari, M. (1966). Financial ratios as a means of forecasting bankruptcy. *Management International Review, 4*, 15–21.

The Bankruptcy Abuse Prevention and Consumer Protection Act of 2005 (BAPCPA) (Pub.L. 109–8, 119 Stat. 23, enacted April 20, 2005), *Changes to the United States Bankruptcy Code.*

The Bankruptcy Reform Act of 1978 (Pub.L. 95–598, 92 Stat. 2549, November 6, 1978), *United States Act of Congress.*

Theodossiou, P., Kahya, E., Saidi, R., & Philippatos, G. (1996). Financial distress and corporate acquisitions: Further empirical evidence. *Journal of Business Finance & Accounting, 23*(5–6), 699–719.

Theodossiou, P. T. (1993). Predicting shifts in the mean of a multivariate time series process: An application in predicting business failures. *Journal of the American Statistical Association, 88*(422), 441–449.

Thietart, R. A., & Vivas, R. (1984). An empirical investigation of success strategies for businesses along the product life cycle. *Management Science, 30*(12), 1405–1423.

Thorburn, K. S. (2000). Bankruptcy auctions: Costs, debt recovery, and firm survival. *Journal of Financial Economics, 58*(3), 337–368.

Tinoco, M. H., & Wilson, N. (2013). Financial distress and bankruptcy prediction among listed companies using accounting, market and macroeconomic variables. *International Review of Financial Analysis, 30*, 394–419.

Tirole, J. (1986). Hierarchies and bureaucracies: On the role of collusion in organizations. *Journal of Law, Economics, and Organization, 2*(2), 181–214.

Titman, S. (1984). The effect of capital structure on a firm's liquidation decision. *Journal of Financial Economics, 13*(1), 137–151.

Trieschmann, J. S., & Pinches, G. E. (1973). A multivariate model for predicting financially distressed PL insurers. *The Journal of Risk and Insurance, 40*, 327–338.

Van De Velde, M. (1987). *Verklaring van de Missclassificaties bij Falingspredicitie.* Dissertation, Department of Business and Finance, University of Ghent.

Verikas, A., Kalsyte, Z., Bacauskiene, M., & Gelzinis, A. (2010). Hybrid and ensemble-based soft computing techniques in bankruptcy prediction: A survey. *Soft Computing, 14*(9), 995–1010.

Warren, C. S. (1980). Uniformity of auditing standards: A replication. *Journal of Accounting Research, 18*, 312–324.

Watts, R. L., & Zimmerman, J. L. (1983). Agency problems, auditing, and the theory of the firm: Some evidence. *The Journal of Law and Economics, 26*(3), 613–633.

Wennberg, K., & DeTienne, D. R. (2014). What do we really mean when we talk about 'exit'? A critical review of research on entrepreneurial exit. *International Small Business Journal, 32*(1), 4–16.

Whitaker, R. B. (1999). The early stages of financial distress. *Journal of Economics and Finance, 23*(2), 123–132.

Wilson, R. L., & Sharda, R. (1994). Bankruptcy prediction using neural networks. *Decision Support Systems, 11*(5), 545–557.

Wruck, K. H. (1990). Financial distress, reorganization, and organizational efficiency. *Journal of Financial Economics, 27*(2), 419–444.

Yang, Z. R., Platt, M. B., & Platt, H. D. (1999). Probabilistic neural networks in bankruptcy prediction. *Journal of Business Research, 44*(2), 67–74.

Yu, F., & Yu, X. (2011). Corporate lobbying and fraud detection. *Journal of Financial and Quantitative Analysis, 46*(6), 1865–1891.

Zhang, G., Hu, M. Y., Patuwo, B. E., & Indro, D. C. (1999). Artificial neural networks in bankruptcy prediction: General framework and cross-validation analysis. *European Journal of Operational Research, 116*(1), 16–32.

Zhang, J. (2008). The contracting benefits of accounting conservatism to lenders and borrowers. *Journal of Accounting and Economics, 45*(1), 27–54.

Zhou, L., Lu, D., & Fujita, H. (2015). The performance of corporate financial distress prediction models with features selection guided by domain knowledge and data mining approaches. *Knowledge-Based Systems, 85*, 52–61.

Zmijewski, M. E. (1984). Methodological issues related to the estimation of financial distress prediction models. *Journal of Accounting Research, 22*, 59–82.

CHAPTER 3

Going Concern Evaluation in the US Context: The Respective Roles of Auditors and Managers

Abstract All the alternative types of corporate financial distress entail risks and uncertainties. A company's ability to continue as a going concern must then be assessed in time and in a proper fashion. In the US, going concern assessment has traditionally been the auditors' responsibility, but investors have complained that by the time auditors make the assessment, a failing business is already on the verge of bankruptcy. For this reason, US interested parties have expressed a need for accounting literature that clarifies that an entity has the primary responsibility for assessing its own ability to continue as a going concern. The chapter analyses a sample of US distressed companies to examine the timeliness of going concern decisions and examines the content evolutions of US accounting and auditing standards.

Keywords Accounting fraud • Albert Dunlap • Collusion • Merger and acquisition • Survival analysis

3.1 Evolution of Going Concern Assessment in the US Context

All the alternative types of corporate financial distress entail risks and uncertainties for the several parties who have different interests in a distressed firm. A company's ability to continue as a going concern must then be monitored and assessed in time and in a proper fashion. During recent decades, going concern evaluation has progressively acquired importance and become a hot topic of discussion for two main reasons: the increasing information flow in the global capital markets, and a series of accounting and financial scandals. The most remarkable scandal in the US capital market was the 2001 Enron Corporation accounting scandal. Enron and its auditor Arthur Andersen used accounting mechanisms to perpetrate an accounting fraud. By exploiting loopholes, it was able to make its financial statements seem profitable and stable: profits continued to be registered in spite of transactions that actually led to heavy losses. Enron is considered an emblematic case of the scandal season, together with WorldCom and Lehman Brothers' scandals. Since the beginning of the financial scandals' season in 2001 and the financial crisis that started at the end of 2007, there has been an increase in the demand for information quality to be reflected in both accounting and auditing standards. In particular, the financial reporting framework provided by US GAAP (i.e. Generally Accepted Accounting Principles) has started to be considered inadequate to analyse corporate financial distress and failure (Beaver et al. 2005). This has been partially propelled by the fact that the increasing complexity of US GAAP has jeopardized their broad and international acceptance (Mirza and Ankarath 2012). This paragraph aims to review and understand the evolution of US accounting and auditing standards, in relation to going concern evaluation of distressed firms.

Considering firstly accounting standards, the US GAAP framework is the result of the efforts of the Financial Accounting Standard Board (FASB), the Emerging Issues Task Force (EITF), the American Institute of Certified Public Accountants (AICPA), and other authoritative bodies. The FASB is one of the components of a non-profit standard-setting group (Angeloni 2016) including the Financial Accounting Foundation (FAF), the Financial Accounting Standards Advisory Council (FASAC), the Governmental Accounting Standards Board (GASB), and the Governmental Accounting Standards Advisory Council (GASAC). Moreover, the FASB's work is influenced by the Securities and Exchange Commission (SEC): this authority supersedes the US GAAP for public companies and regulates the form and content of financial statements (Shamrock 2012). US financial statements are also regulated by many interpretations and bulletins (EITF Statements, AICPA Statements of Position, and SEC guidance). Although the setting of accounting standards is not limited to one entity, the "ultimate authority to set accounting rules and reporting requirements rests with the US Congress, the SEC and, as it is typical for a common-law regime, the rulings set out by the courts" (Hail et al. 2010, p. 368). Financial reporting quality depends both on such accounting rules and on the audit quality. If the audit quality is high, then the credibility of the financial reports will increase. This credibility derives from the greater assurance that the financial statements faithfully reflect the business's underlying economy.

From an auditing point of view, the abovementioned AICPA represents the Certified Public Accountant (CPA) profession. The AICPA is charged with developing auditing standards for private companies and other professional organizations in order to provide guidance to its members. It is also charged with issuing interpretations and other guidelines for users of auditing standards. The Auditing Standards Board (ASB) is the AICPA's senior committee. Its mission is to serve the public interest through the development and updating of Statements on Auditing Standards (SAS). Focusing on going concern evaluation, in 1981 the AICPA published SAS No. 34, entitled "The Auditor's Considerations When Question Arises About an Entity's Continued Existence". Before that date, there was no literature on the issue of substantial doubt until the entity existed. Under this standard, a going concern opinion was assured unless there was quantitative and observable evidence of the opposite (Levitan and Knoblett 1985). SAS No. 34 was followed by SAS No. 54, which addressed the auditors' responsibility for detecting misstatements resulting from illegal acts[1]: this second auditing standard, like the previous one, was of poor economic value being virtually meaningless and using ambiguous language. In 1988 the AICPA published SAS No. 59, entitled "The Auditor's Consideration of an Entity's Ability to Continue as a Going Concern". Since its issuance, the aim has clearly been to involve auditors in a more serious way in order to make their opinions more accountable. SAS No. 59 was superseded by SAS No. 126 (illustrated in the last paragraph of this chapter) in June 2012, and therefore after the accounting financial scandals examined in the next paragraph. For that reason, we will outline here the content of SAS No. 59 to introduce the next empirical investigation.

---

[1] Although auditors were not required to search for any kind of illegal acts, SAS No. 54 did obligate auditors to notify senior management and the board if evidence of an illegal act was discovered. Specifically, SAS No. 54 and "Illegal Acts by Clients", AU Section 317.03 of the AICPA Professional Standards, stated: "Whether an act is, in fact, illegal is a determination that is normally beyond the auditor's professional competence. An auditor, in reporting on financial statements, presents himself as one who is proficient in accounting and auditing. The auditor's training experience and understanding of the client and its industry may provide for recognition that some client acts coming to his attention may be illegal. However, the determination as to whether a particular act is illegal would generally be based on the advice of an informed expert qualified to practice law or may have to await final determination by a court of law."

This auditing standard (SAS No. 59) assumed that financial statements were not being prepared using the liquidation basis of accounting. Compared to SAS No. 34, SAS No. 59 introduced three main changes. First, auditors had to consider the client's going concern status for every audit engagement. Second, the audit report was to be modified if there was substantial doubt regarding the firm's going concern status. Specifically, according to AU Section 341 (entitled "The Auditor's Consideration of an Entity's Ability to Continue as a Going Concern"), auditors were charged to evaluate any substantial doubt over a reasonable period of time, which meant not exceeding 12 months beyond the date of the financial statement being audited. Third, the audit report was to include an explanatory paragraph regarding the substantial doubt (Asare 1990). Auditors' evaluations were based on their ability to assess conditions or events existing or that occurred before the date of the audit report. In addition, the standard listed what auditors should have implemented in order to evaluate the substantial doubt and the related events before the issuance of their report. Auditors had to consider the aggregate results of activities carried out during the planning, the collection of audit evidence to achieve the audit objectives, and the audit activities in completion of the auditing. Paragraph 5 of SAS No. 59 stated that the audit procedures to identify if substantial doubt existed should not have been ad hoc procedures because the results of the usual audit procedures (relevant to other audit objectives) should have been sufficient to recognize conditions and events. The standards listed some examples of such audit procedures: analytical procedures, review of subsequent events, or reading of minutes concerning the meetings of stockholders or board of directors. Auditors were required to consider the conditions and events in the aggregate and pay attention to circumstances in which these conditions and events occurred. Even in this case, the standard listed some examples of events divided for macro classes: negative trends, signals of possible financial difficulties, internal and external matters. The audit procedures relating to subsequent events helpful to identifying events that may have contributed to a conclusion that substantial doubt existed had to be considered in order to complete the auditing evaluation. The duration of the evaluation period depended on each audit requirement following the period of specific audit activities: the same procedure could have been carried out before or after the balance sheet date. Some other audit procedures were applicable only after the balance sheet date since data were not available before. These procedures included the evaluation of cut-offs and data providing helpful information for assets' and liabilities' evaluations on the balance sheet date. Other procedures relating to the subsequent events were required in order to evaluate if adjustments or more disclosure were needed for a fair presentation of the financial statement. These procedures should have been performed near or on the date of the auditor's report. In particular the auditors should have read the last interim financial statement and compared it with the financial statement being reported upon. In order to complete the audit procedures, auditors should have questioned management in the accounting and financial areas about any significant changes that could have affected the values of the financial statement under audit. Such enquiries should have concerned the capital stock, long-term debt, or working capital as well as the current status of assets. Moreover, officers should have obtained information about any unusual adjustment applied from the balance sheet date to the date of inquiry. Another activity auditors should have performed to obtain information about the subsequent events concerned was to have read the minutes of the meetings of stockholders, as well as directors and committees, in order to highlight hypothetical events that could have led to significant changes in the financial statement under audit. In the event that the auditors judged that evidence pointed to the presence of substantial doubt, firstly, they should have obtained additional information about the management's plans to alleviate substantial doubt; secondly, they should have estimated their possible implementation. Since its issuance and until the accounting scandals recalled in the next paragraph, SAS No. 59 was considered something of a guarantee for investors. Since those scandals, both accounting and audit standard setters have been involved in projects aiming to review the standards.

3.2   TIMELINESS OF GOING CONCERN DECISIONS

The previous paragraph focuses on the evolution of US standards about the evaluation of corporate going concern before the abovementioned "scandals season" from 2001. The latest developments of such standards, analysed in the last paragraph of this chapter, were sought by several parties, especially by investors. They had complained that by the time auditors make the going concern assessment, a business may already be on the verge of bankruptcy or a delisting from its stock exchange. The present paragraph aims to explore this complaint that will then be empirically verified in the next paragraph. The complaint relates to the change of auditors' opinion (from unqualified to qualified). Auditors without any reservations about the financial statements give an unqualified opinion. This states that auditors feel the company followed all accounting rules appropriately and that the financial reports are an accurate representation of the company's financial condition. It is the opposite of qualified auditor's opinion when the financial status of a distressed firm is uncertain. Auditors have the responsibility to evaluate whether there is substantial doubt about the firm's ability to continue as a going concern for a reasonable period of time, as emphasized in the previous paragraph. Such evaluations are based on the knowledge of relevant conditions and events obtained from the auditing procedures performed during a financial statement audit. Auditors' timeliness in issuing a qualified opinion represents the root of the complaint and of the recent developments of (accounting and auditing) standards. Several causes may influence such timeliness and give rise to some research questions with different hypotheses, as described in the following.

The first research question relates the timing of auditors' evaluation to the corporate path of financial distress.

RQ 1 : When do auditors issue qualified opinions during the corporate path of financial distress?

The timing of corporate financial distress is explored in the second chapter: while there is abundant literature describing prediction models of corporate bankruptcy, fewer research contributions have sought to predict corporate financial distress. This lack is related to the difficulty in defining the onset of financial distress: it is due to the indeterminacy regarding when a firm becomes financially distressed. Most studies which purport to focus on financial distress, instead, examine only the terminal date associated with the company's filing for bankruptcy protection because that date is definitive (Platt and Platt 2002). The present work identifies some steps in the corporate financial distress process. This is a dangerous (Sun and Li 2011), but not always fatal (Platt and Platt 2002) path that may characterize a corporate life cycle and generally starts after a micro-failure, as emphasized in the second chapter. A firm may either recover its financial situation where the distress is temporary (Donovan et al. 2015; Zhang 2008) or embark on a failure path because of worsening financial distress. Corporate financial distress, therefore, envisages two alternatives (i.e. successful recovery or failure). Failure is a fatal path in that its final outcome entails a radical change for the failing firm. This final step is called macro-failure (Agostini 2013) here and may be defined in different ways "as the stochastic events that finally pull the rug away from under the tottering firm. A picturesque but by no means unhelpful analogy is that of the drunkard rolling along the cliff edge in the face of a gale with the actual event being represented by the gust which finally blow him over" (Taffler 1982, pp. 354–355). In the empirical analysis implemented in the next paragraph, three types of macro-failure are considered: bankruptcy (Chap. 11), merger, and acquisition. The identification of these steps within the path of corporate financial distress allows us to introduce a hypothesis in response to the first research question to verify the complaint about the timeliness of auditors' going concern decision.

H1 : By the time the auditors make their assessment concerning the ability of a distressed firm to continue as a going concern, the business is closer to a macro-failure than to a micro-failure.

An auditor's going concern evaluation consists of two stages (Krishnan and Krishnan 1996): auditors evaluate information to form an initial impression of an entity's financial condition and then decide on the type of audit report to be issued. Referring to DeAngelo's (1981) definition of audit quality, while the first stage depends on auditors' competence, the second stage and auditors' final decision depend on their independence. Acting as rational economic agents, auditors may be influenced by the perceived consequences of issuing a going concern report (DeAngelo 1981; Watts and Zimmerman 1983). Risk of litigation, risk of loss of reputation, and risk of loss of business are factors suggested in the literature which may relate to the economic trade-offs faced by the auditor (Krishnan and Krishnan 1996). Consequently, these factors could influence the auditor's going concern opinion decision. Loss of business following the issuance of a going concern opinion can occur due to auditor switching or due to clients' macro-failure. The belief that a client will go bankrupt as a result of a going concern uncertainty disclosure in the audit report is known in the literature as the self-fulfilling prophecy hypothesis (Mutchler 1985). The risk of litigation and risk of loss of reputation may have a positive effect on auditor independence, while the risk of business loss may compromise auditor independence. In particular, the working together of managers and auditors is especially relevant for going concern evaluation, as emphasized in the second chapter. Auditors' evaluation may benefit from the work of actors having more updated and relevant information at their disposal, but there may also be a risk of collusion. The analysis of this relation between managers and auditors regarding going concern evaluation is especially relevant for defining their reciprocal responsibilities, understanding the abovementioned investors' complaint, and explaining the recent developments of US (accounting and auditing) standards.

RQ 2 : Management assessment and auditors' decision about going concern: which is issued first?

In the second chapter, corporate financial distress is described using two criteria: its type (i.e. either temporary or severe) and its representation in financial statements (i.e. either fair or fraudulent). The first criterion has been touched on in the first research question, while the second is used here to analyse the temporal alignment of managers' assessment and auditors' evaluation about going concern. We will investigate the interdependence between management's and auditors' going concern assessments, by distinguishing between fraud and no-tort cases. If the auditors' evaluation is efficient, then fraud cases will be discovered in time and before management disclosure. In fraud cases, then, there should be disagreement between management's and auditors' going concern assessments.

H2a : In fraud cases, auditors' going concern decision precedes management assessment.

H2b : In no-tort cases, auditors' going concern decision does not precede management assessment.

In order to examine the timeliness of going concern decisions and answer our two research questions, the next paragraph analyses a sample of US distressed companies.

3.3   ANALYSIS, OBSERVATIONS, AND RESULTS

The analysis implemented in this paragraph begins by investigating the timeliness of going concern evaluations during corporate financial distress paths in order to answer the research questions described in the previous paragraph.

Concerning the distinction between temporary and severe corporate financial distress, the analysis initially focuses on severe corporate financial distress that leads to macro-failure. The investigated sample (Table 3.1) includes all the US fraud cases mentioned by the UCLA–LoPucki

Table 3.1   The investigated sample, including all the US fraud cases (and the matched no-tort cases) mentioned by the UCLA–LoPucki Bankruptcy Research Database, acting in a SIC code division different from the H and filing for bankruptcy between 1991 and March 1, 2010

	All fraud cases mentioned by the UCLA–LoPucki Bankruptcy Research Database	Year of filing	SIC code	Benchmarks (selection of competitors)
1	Adelphia Business Solutions, Inc.	2002	48	ITC DeltaCom, Inc.
2	Adelphia Communications Corp.	2002	48	IMPSAT Fiber Networks, Inc.
3	American Banknote Corporation	1999	27	MediaNews Group Inc.
4	American Tissue, Inc.	2001	26	American Pad & Paper Company
5	Anicom, Inc.	2001	50	Inacom Corp.
6	Aurora Foods Inc.	2003	20	Interstate Bakeries Corporation
7	Bonneville Pacific Corporation	1991	16	Morrison Knudsen Corp.
8	Boston Chicken, Inc.	1998	58	Flagstar Companies Inc.
9	CareMatrix Corp.	2000	83	Sun HealthCare Group, Inc.
10	Complete Management, Inc.	1999	87	ProMedCo Management Company
11	Enron Corp.	2001	51	KCS Energy, Inc.
12	Fine Host Corporation	1999	58	Planet Hollywood International Inc.
13	Footstar Inc.	2004	56	Jacobson Stores, Inc.
14	Global Crossing Ltd.	2002	48	Global TeleSystems, Inc.
15	Impath Inc.	2003	80	aaiPharma Inc.
16	Leslie Fay Companies, Inc.	1993	23	Plaid Clothing Group Inc.
17	MCSI Inc.	2003	50	CHS Electronics, Inc.
18	MobileMedia Communications, Inc.	1997	48	Geotek Communications, Inc.
19	OCA, Inc.	2006	80	Mediq, Inc.
20	Peregrine Systems, Inc.	2002	73	USInterNetworking, Inc.
21	Philip Services Corp. (1999)	1999	49	Waste Systems International, Inc.
22	Seitel Inc.	2003	13	Forcenergy, Inc.
23	Seven Seas Petroleum, Inc.	2002	13	Coho Energy, Inc. (2002)
24	Smartalk Teleservices, Inc.	1999	73	GST Telecommunications, Inc.
25	Sunbeam Corporation	2001	36	Sun Television and Appliances, Inc.
26	Washington Group International, Inc.	2001	15	WCI Communities, Inc.
27	Worldcom, Inc.	2002	48	XO Communications, Inc.

Bankruptcy Research Database[2], acting in a Standard Industrial Classification (SIC) code division different from the H[3] and filing for bankruptcy between 1991 and March 1, 2010.

Several factors explain why a set of bankrupt firms provides a useful sample through which to examine auditors' judgements. In particular, bankruptcy represents the most reliable and objective type of macro-failure: bankrupt companies have experienced a failing path of severe financial distress. Therefore, for each sample firm, auditors should have modified going concern reports at some point before the macro-failure. Some financial deterioration of the firm must have occurred before the actual bankruptcy filing, suggesting that alert auditors should have begun revising their going concern opinions well in advance of the bankruptcy announcement. Regarding the representation of corporate financial distress in the annual accounts, the analysis considers both fair and fraudulent representations. Indeed, limiting the investigated sample only to firms perpetrating fraud would probably introduce a selection bias since auditors may not have perceived management's true opinion about their firms' going concern status. The construction of a matched sample of no-tort firms with similar activities and comparable levels of severe financial distress (since we know that they are heading towards bankruptcy) provides a benchmark against which to evaluate the assessment provided by management for those firms that ultimately go bankrupt. For this reason, each sampled firm has been matched with another US firm identified by the UCLA–LoPucki Bankruptcy Research Database as a no-tort case of bankruptcy. The selection has been based on three further conditions which are the period of filing for bankruptcy, the SIC code, and the description of business. These are the same criteria used by Mergent's database in the identification of competitors. Companies' details (such as business description, history, and subsidiaries), annual reports, and other financial data were also analysed for the matched firms. This selection approach provides an initial characterization of the sampled firms and allows interesting comparisons of auditors'

---

[2] UCLA–LoPucki Bankruptcy Research is a data collection, data linking, and data dissemination project of the University of California, Los Angeles, School of Law (UCLA School of Law). This database contains data on all large, public company bankruptcy cases filed in the US Bankruptcy Courts.

[3] The SIC code division called H identifies finance, insurance, and real estate activities. Companies belonging to division H (in the financial, real estate, and insurance sectors) have been removed from the sample because these types of companies are supposed to have unique financial features and specific regulations.

going concern opinions: the analysis of auditors' opinions for firms perpetrating fraud against their matched firm counterparts allows us to control for possible selection bias and provides interesting data about the timeliness of auditors' decisions for financially distressed firms.

The analysis of such timeliness requires, first of all, the identification of micro-failures according to the categories described in the second chapter. The relevant micro-failure (Agostini 2013) is identified for each sampled firm: it corresponds to the stage of not meeting certain objectives which influences the firm's path towards macro-failure because of imposing a drastic choice, either revealing or not revealing its negative consequences. The identification of the relevant micro-failures for all the sampled firms (for both the fraud and no-tort cases) has been made with the help of form 10-Ks.[4] Content analysis has been implemented in order to identify micro-failures and categorize them according to the mentioned categories (Table 3.2). This represents a well-established method in the social sciences (Jones and Shoemaker 1994; Boyatzis 1998; Holsti 1969; Krippendorff 1980; Weber 1985). The results (Agostini 2013) show that accidental factors (i.e. category E) have no influence at all on firms' relevant micro-failures. Moreover, neither categories A (product/market problems) nor D (cultural/social factors) have much influence. Furthermore, there is a strict differentiation within these micro-failure types according to the representation of corporate financial distress in annual accounts: in no-tort cases financial micro-failures outnumber managerial problems and vice versa in fraud cases. More specifically, while in no-tort cases financial micro-failures outnumber all the others, in fraud cases the managerial relevant micro-failure type is the prevalent one.

After the identification of the relevant micro-failures, a survival analysis has been implemented to investigate the timing of going concern evaluations in the distressed companies' paths to macro-failure. In order to implement the survival analysis a time variable has been introduced: this represents the time interval between the relevant micro-failure date and macro-failure date. Thus, this variable is not calculated from the beginning

---

[4] Forms 10-K are annual reports required by the US SEC that give a comprehensive summary of each public company's performance. The 10-K includes information such as company history, organizational structure, executive compensation, equity, subsidiaries, and audited financial statements. Forms 10-K, as well as other SEC filings, have been searched at the EDGAR database on the SEC's website. In addition to the 10-K, which is filed annually, other data have been downloaded. In fact, in the period between these filings, and in case of a significant event, such as a CEO departing or bankruptcy, a Form 8-K must be filed in order to provide up-to-date information.

Table 3.2 Micro-failures categorization according to the traditional clusters

---

A. *Product/market problems*
   A1. Competition and/or competitors with significantly greater financial resources than the company
   A2. Customers' criticism because of goods quality (either too expensive or too low quality)
   A3. Depressed industry and market downturn
   A4. New and stricter industry regulations
   A5. Seasonal business
B. *Financial problems*
   B1. Excessive costs and/or additional and non-essential expenses
   B2. Excessive indebtedness and difficulty in obtaining new financing
   B3. Investors' nervousness, bad relationship with venture capitalists, and/or creditors' pressure
   B4. Negative economic–financial trends (primarily a decrease in revenues)
   B5. Relationship of strong financial dependence with other player(s) (suppliers, customers, …)
   B6. Unprofitable ventures (e.g. acquisition of unprofitable divisions)
C. *Managerial/key employee problems*
   C1. Conflicts of interest
   C2. Core business abandonment and diversification into other industries
   C3. Excessive anxiety to keep up with increasingly large competitors
   C4. Important decisions made without obtaining board approval
   C5. Legal, apparently correct, but improper (e.g. deficit analytical) accountancy
   C6. Poor management and disengaged board
   C7. Principals' legal problems unconnected with the firm
   C8. Private benefits (withdrawals, bonuses, and compensation policy)
   C9. Too aggressive growth and expansion strategy (i.e. too rapid growth through mergers or other operations proving unsustainable in the long run)
   C10. Too ambitious objectives and anxiety to hit "must make" figures (i.e. earnings targets)
   C11. Mistaken operations (because of riskiness or other reasons)
D. *Cultural/social factors*
   D1. Corruption
   D2. Discrimination problems
   D3. Powerful enemies
E. *Accidental factors*
   E1. Calamities

---

of the business path, but from its relevant micro-failure, which is the most reliable signal of the status of corporate financial distress. The path towards macro-failure of the sampled firms ranges from 215 days (the minimum value) to 2722 days (the maximum value). The minimum and the maximum values of the time variable are lower for no-tort cases. Moreover, the range between these last two values is shorter for no-tort cases: firms which have committed fraud are more distributed over time and their paths towards macro-failure last longer. Even though overall the path towards macro-failure lasts longer for fraud cases, after the disclosure moment firms that have committed fraud fall into macro-failure more rapidly than no-tort firms. In short, after the relevant micro-failure, macro-failure occurs more quickly in no-tort cases, but after the disclosure moment, macro-failure occurs really quickly in fraud cases (Agostini 2013).

The analysis of the timeliness of auditors' going concern evaluations requires the introduction of a further date in the survival function. The year of auditors' last unqualified report would seem to fit the case: this is the last year to which financial statements refer without auditors' substantial doubt about the ability of the entity to remain a going concern. For instance, if the annual report refers to the accounting period starting January 1, 2009, and ending December31, 2009, and in 2010 auditors have issued the last unqualified going concern opinion about the 2009 financial situation, the recorded year will assume a value equal to 2009. Starting from this year (in order to establish an objective datum), then, the auditors' qualified opinion has been recorded one year later when auditors state in their audit reports that there is substantial doubt about the ability of the distressed company to continue as a going concern. The variable called *time1* corresponds to the number of years between the relevant micro-failure and auditors' assessment, while the variable called *time2* refers to the number of years between auditors' assessment and the final macro-failure. These have been compared. Some descriptive statistics have been calculated for both (Table 3.3).

This first analysis reveals some difference between *time1* and *time2* values. First of all, the minimum value assumed by *time1* variable (i.e. the number of years between the relevant micro-failure and auditors' assessment) is 0 because there is one case (out of 54) in which auditors' assessment year coincides with the relevant micro-failure occurrence. For this reason, the survival function considers only 53 cases for the variable *time1*. The analysis of the *time2* variable (i.e. the number of years between auditors' assessment and the final macro-failure) refers to only 15 cases (out of 54) because in 39 cases auditors did not issue qualified opinions before the macro-failure. The survival functions (Fig. 3.1) estimate about a 75% chance that *time1* equals 3 years and *time2* equals 2 years: the difference is still more relevant if we differentiate fraud and no-tort cases.

Table 3.3   Descriptive statistical analysis of *time1* and *time2* variables

Variables	Obs	Mean	Std. dev.	Min	Max
time1	54	2.351852	1.402927	0	7
time2	54	0.3518519	0.7808415	0	3

Variables	Survival analyses						
			incidence	no. of	├──── Survival time ────┤		
time1		time at risk	rate	subjects	25%	50%	75%
	total	126	.4206349	53	1	2	3
			incidence	no. of	├──── Survival time ────┤		
time2		time at risk	rate	subjects	25%	50%	75%
	total	21	.7142857	15	1	1	2

Fig. 3.1   Survival analyses for both *time1* and *time2* variables

Variables	Survival analyses							
				incidence	no. of	├──── Survival time ────┤		
	fraud	time at risk		rate	subjects	25%	50%	75%
time1	0	46		.5652174	26	1	2	2
	1	80		.3375	27	2	3	4
	total	126		.4206349	53	1	2	3
				incidence	no. of	├──── Survival time ────┤		
	fraud	time at risk		rate	subjects	25%	50%	75%
time2	0	5		1	5	1	1	1
	1	16		.625	10	1	1	2
	total	21		.7142857	15	1	1	2

Fig. 3.2   Survival analysis for both *time1* and *time2* variables distinguishing between no-tort and fraud cases

Especially in fraud cases[5] (Fig. 3.2), the *time1* variable assumes values significantly greater than the *time2* variable: the functions estimate about a 50% chance that *time1* equals 3 years and *time2* equals 1 year. There appears to be about a 75% chance that *time1* equals 4 years and *time2* equals 2 years.

The timeliness of auditors' qualified opinions is now compared with the timing of management assessments. This comparison raises some considerations. The relevant micro-failure represents a reliable signal of corpo-

[5] The variable *fraud* equals 0 in no-tort cases and 1 in fraudulent cases.

rate financial distress. In no-tort cases firms' economic downturn is more evident because a negative management assessment reveals those negative consequences. Therefore, in no-tort cases, relevant micro-failure date coincides with management assessment year. On the other hand, in fraud cases, the disclosure of the fraud identifies the date in which the firm economic downturn is revealed by the management. For these reasons, the comparison between auditors' and management's timing is differentiated among fraud and no-tort cases. In fraud cases, the variable called *time2_fraud* corresponds to the number of years between auditors' assessment and macro-failure in fraud cases, while the variable called *time3_fraud* refers to the number of years between the disclosure moment and the final macro-failure in fraud cases. These have been compared. Descriptive statistics (Table 3.4) suggest that management evaluation and auditors' assessment are close in the failing path of firms perpetrating fraud: both the variables' means and ranges (between maximum and minimum values) seem to affirm the same.

In no-tort cases, the variable called *time2_notort* refers to the number of years between auditors' assessment and the final macro-failure, while the variable called *time3_notort* corresponds to the number of years between management assessment and the final macro-failure. Descriptive statistics (Table 3.5) suggest that auditors' negative going concern decisions are prompter than management assessments, after firms' negative economic downturn has been clearly revealed.

Table 3.4 Descriptive statistical analysis of both *time2_fraud* and *time3_fraud* variables

Variables	Obs	Mean	Std. dev.	Min	Max
time2_fraud	27	0.5185185	1.014145	0	3
time3_fraud	27	0.5925926	0.8439495	0	3

Table 3.5 Descriptive statistical analysis of both *time2_notort* and *time3_notort* variables

Variables	Obs	Mean	Std. dev.	Min	Max
time2_notort	27	0.1851852	0.3958474	0	1
time3_notort	27	1.888889	0.9336996	1	5

The illustrated descriptive statistics and survival functions highlight the existence of a precise temporal relation between management's assessment and auditors' opinion about the capability of distressed companies to continue as going concern in both fraud and no-tort cases. They represent a first attempt to analyse the temporal evolution of auditors' going concern opinions based on a set of distressed firms including all the US fraud cases, mentioned by the UCLA–LoPucki Bankruptcy Research Database and acting in a division different from the H, that filed for bankruptcy during the period 1991–2010 and a corresponding set of industry-matched firms that did not perpetrate fraud. The survival functions demonstrate that fraud lets distressed firms earn time in their path towards macro-failure, but its disclosure makes distressed firms tip towards macro-failure very fast. Both management's and auditors' assessments about going concern are closer to macro-failure rather than to the micro-failure that first indicates a clear status of corporate financial distress.

Going deeper, five examined cases change the auditing firm during the analysed corporate financial paths (between the relevant micro-failure and the macro-failure): such changes occurred three years before macro-failure in three cases, two years before macro-failure only in one case and one year before macro-failure again only once. Moreover, the survival analysis of the time between the relevant micro-failure date and the fraud disclosure date does not signal any outliers: none of the examined fraud cases present values significantly far from the median survival time which has been estimated as equal to 1182 days.

On the other hand, the survival analysis of the time between the fraud disclosure date and the macro-failure date (Fig. 3.3) reaches the opposite conclusion and reveals the presence of an outlier. Overall, the function estimates about a 25% chance of macro-failure collapse within 53 days after the fraud disclosure date, 50% within 99 days, and 75% within 215 days. On the basis of some descriptive statistics, the maximum value of the variable is estimated as equal to 840 days (Agostini and Favero

	time at risk	incidence rate	no. of subjects	Survival time 25%	50%	75%
total	4646	.0062419	29	53	99	215

Fig. 3.3 Survival analysis of the time between the fraud disclosure date and the date of macro-failure

Table 3.6   Relevant steps in Sunbeam Corp's path of financial distress

Fraud case emerged as outlier	Relevant micro-failure (date)	Fraud disclosure (date)	Auditors' qualified opinion (year)	Macro-failure (date)
Sunbeam Corporation	September 30, 1996	October 20, 1998	1998	February 6, 2001

←————————————————→	←————————————————→
750 days between the relevant micro-failure and the fraud disclosure	840 days between the fraud disclosure and the macro-failure

2017): this is well outside the range estimated by the survival function and it refers to *Sunbeam Corp.* (hereafter called Sunbeam). This case emerges as an outlier in the examined sample because of the unusual temporal length to total macro-failure after the disclosure of Sunbeam's fraud (Table 3.6).

Given the exceptionality of the case, even in the light of existing literature on the determinants and characteristics of accounting fraud, an in-depth study of Sunbeam's path to macro-failure has been carried out (Agostini and Favero 2017), with the aim of explaining (Cybinski 2001; Humphrey 2008) the reasons for its uniqueness, the micro-analysis raising new questions and considerations concerning corporate financial distress in cases of accounting fraud. Certain unique features elude aggregate statistical analysis: the case of Sunbeam Corp., presented here, questions the regularities identified by statistical analysis. A micro-analytical approach was able to trace the complex dynamics of that case and to explain Sunbeam's exceptionally long trajectory to macro-failure. It highlights three main factors characterizing the case: the specific corporate path of financial distress, the role of managers, and auditors' ascribed responsibilities (Agostini and Favero 2017).

The first point concerns the peculiar modality of fraud disclosure and the subsequent board reaction. Albert J. Dunlap (hereafter simply called Dunlap) became Sunbeam's CEO in 1996 when the company was in a situation of financial distress particularly on account of poor performance in the early 1990s and a lost lawsuit against the former CEO, fired in 1992. It was hoped that Dunlap's arrival at the company would lead to an exit from the corporate financial distress path. In order to restructure the distressed company, Dunlap adopted an aggressive managerial strategy: he ordered massive cuts to product lines, plants, and employees, urged his subordinates to do whatever they could to reach almost impossible targets on pain of dismissal, while also offering them much larger rewards in stock options than any other company if they met their goals (Agostini and Favero 2017). This part of his aggressive restructuring behaviour was visible and evident to all the stakeholders, but it was not the only stratagem implemented. Indeed, Dunlap, together with a few close collaborators, also orchestrated a fraudulent scheme to create the illusion of a successful restructuring of Sunbeam. His eventual aim was the sale of the company at an inflated price, but this mission failed, and that unsuccessful event was the starting point of a fall in Sunbeam's stock that in 1998 arrived at its minimum value of US$22 per share following the tumble in profits. This negative situation sparked considerable interest: an analyst from *Barron's Online* analysed Sunbeam's path of financial distress and disclosed that it had actually realized a negative operating cash flow in 1997, insinuating the implementation of questionable accounting practices. Following that first disclosure, many different fraudulent accounting techniques emerged, which had been implemented over the course of Sunbeam's fraud from October 1996 to June 1998. The main fraudulent loopholes consisted in boosting accounts receivable (through so-called channel stuffing[6]), accounting fictitious sales (through "the improper recording of bill-and-hold sales", SEC 2001), and "cookie jar" reserves[7]. After the disclosure of such ploys, Dunlap was immediately accused of sole responsibility for Sunbeam's fraud and he was forced to resign. This CEO scapegoating (Agostini and Favero 2017), in spite of fraud disclosure, permitted the new corporate board to gain more time before macro-failure, than in the usual corporate paths of financial distress.

CEO scapegoating introduces *a second point relevant to auditing and going concern evaluation*. Arthur Andersen LLP was in charge of the Sunbeam audit. This company was one of the "Big Five" auditing firms—now the "Big Four" (KPMG, Deloitte Touche Tohmatsu, PricewaterhouseCoopers, and Ernst & Young) because Arthur Andersen was found guilty of criminal charges after the famous Enron's

[6] Channel stuffing consists in recording inventory as shipped before delivery or final acceptance. It is a loophole that inflates sales and earnings figures by deliberately sending retailers more products than they are able to sell to the public.

[7] Cookie jar reserves are sums set aside to shore up profits in lean years. They are used to smooth out volatility in corporate financial results, thus giving investors the misleading impression that the company is consistently meeting earnings targets.

bankruptcy in 2001. Before the latter events, however, it audited Sunbeam's financial statements. It discovered some of the recorded fraudulent transactions, especially those related to the so-called spare-parts gambit (Norris 2001a): Sunbeam Corp. had signed an "agreement to agree" with the company EPI Printer that bought a lot of Sunbeam's spare parts, paying US$11 million. Thanks to this transaction, Sunbeam recorded a profit of US$8 million before the end of 1997, knowing that EPI Printer could withdraw from the sale at the beginning of the following year because of an escape clause in the initial agreement. Phillip E. Harlow, the Arthur Andersen partner in charge of the Sunbeam audit, discovered some of the fraudulent accounting transactions and convinced Dunlap to reduce the false profit from US$8 million to US$5 million. The residue was considered "not material" by the auditor. This verged on the acceptable according to an old "rule of thumb" (Jennings et al. 1984): a misstatement was material when its amount was above a predefined threshold level (5–10%) of disclosure. After the definitive discovery of the accounting fraud, the auditing firm justified its work on the basis of "professional disagreements about the application of sophisticated accounting standards" (Norris 2001a), emphasizing the substantial reduction (US$3 million) of "sham profits" (Norris 2001a). Because of the then lack of strict regulation, auditors had only to pay a fine because they had not exercised appropriate scepticism in the Sunbeam case, but could continue to operate (until the Enron case). Thus only Sunbeam's CEO (Dunlap) was scapegoated and banned from ever serving as an officer or director of a public company. Even this limited scapegoating would not have occurred, if the abovementioned corporate sale had been realized. This is related to the third (and last) relevant point about *the events allowing Sunbeam's fraud to be discovered*. Dunlap had planned the sale of the company after having pushed its stock to the maximum value through the described fraudulent loopholes. The sale had two important targets: the end of the fraud path with the definitive concealment of its implementation and the realization of the fictitious value created through such ploys. In spite of several attempts, Sunbeam's sale proved impossible because of the excessively high stock price (Agostini and Favero 2017). Dunlap therefore embarked on a second-best strategy: Sunbeam's acquisition of other three companies permitted a realization of the overvalued stocks of the company, but did not conceal the accounting fraud, as a sale would have done. This suggests the existence of a rating of fraudsters' preference about the types of macro-failure in so far as corporate sale is preferred to acquisition because of a more successful cover-up of fraud implementation.

Al Dunlap was accused in the peculiar case of Sunbeam Corp. of being the main orchestrator of the fraud. It is therefore interesting to consider how his managerial strategy was applied in the companies where he worked before becoming CEO of Sunbeam Corp. in order to verify if similar fraudulent plans went undetected in such cases. Indeed, the failed sale of Sunbeam Corp. suggests that Dunlap's fraudulent scheme might have been successfully applied in his previous working experiences, in particular those concluding with specific types of macro-failure, such as mergers and acquisitions. This points to the usually "invisible" connection between mergers and acquisitions, and fraud (Erickson et al. 2011). The approach of investigating Dunlap's previous working experiences focuses the analysis at the individual level. It is close to the conception of firms as abstractions that exist only in a legal sense and lack decisional capacity (Bradford 2014): firms as such do not decide whether to comply with the law, but individual people, because it is individuals who exercise decisional authority on firms' behalf (Langevoort 2002). Thus, according to the personality theory, in so far as individuals are the decision-makers, they are central to explaining the behaviour of firms, which can be considered as the final result of a chain of causation running through the personalities of such decision-makers. In a theoretical model of corporate legal compliance four constructs in the personalities of CEOs are responsible for firms' compliance or violation of the legal regimes governing corporate behaviour: militarism, anomism, hostility, and adventurism. According to this model, Dunlap is defined as "a militaristic anomist who is hostile and adventuristic" (Bradford 2014, p. 406). The focus on Dunlap's unique personality only emerged in relation to his manoeuvres as CEO at Sunbeam. As we suggested above, it is interesting to consider if his managing style, in particular his fraudulent propensity in the face of corporate financial distress, was also in evidence before Sunbeam. We therefore attempt below a broad reconstruction of Al Dunlap's managerial experiences, using historical information gathered through the database LexisNexis Academic.

Albert J. Dunlap was born in 1937 in Hoboken. He served three years of compulsory military service where he acquired "disciplines, organizational skills, competition and leadership" (Perkins and Wylie 1999). In 1963 he obtained his first job as a trainee in a factory in Wisconsin of *Kimberly-Clark Corporation* (hereafter called Kimberly-

Clark), an American multinational group and world leader in the paper products sector. He assimilated the management style of his boss Frank Nobbe, learning the importance of setting strict standards, demanding maximum performance, being hard on those who are not up to par, being present in the company, and talking to employees, calling them by name. In Kimberly-Clark, Dunlap also gained a strong disregard for managerial bureaucracy as well as a dislike of executives unable to address difficult issues and decisions.

After four years of experience in Kimberly-Clark, Dunlap was hired by *Sterling Pulp & Paper Co.* in 1966 as general manager of the plant in Eau Claire (Wisconsin). The Sterling Pulp & Paper Co. was in financial distress due to the considerable borrowing necessary to purchase the most modern paper and cellulose machineries. In this company Dunlap found himself faced with a number of difficult problems to solve. In his nearly seven years at the helm, Dunlap was credited with having improved labour relations, cut costs, including the dismissal of about a 1000 employees, and increased market share through the development of new products. Dunlap left office when the owner of the Sterling died in June 1973.

In November 1973, *Max Phillips & Sons Inc.*, a rival company of Sterling Pulp & Paper Co. based in Eau Claire, offered him a three-year contract. Here, Dunlap was fired after less than two months. The reasons given for the dismissal were neglect of duties and having spoken disparagingly of the head, jeopardizing the company's business.

After being fired, it took almost six months for Dunlap to find another job. He was hired by another paper mill, *Nitec Paper Corporation* (hereafter called Nitec), again with the burdensome task of reviving the company. The restructuring implemented by Dunlap had the desired effect and brought in two years (from 1974 to 1975) a sharp improvement in the income statement, steadily increasing Nitec's profits. Dunlap earned the esteem of the owner (George Petty) and succeeded in reviving the Nitec Paper Corporation. Although the 1976 results were particularly positive, Petty was forced to dismiss Dunlap over problems of company image and personal relationships with the other managers. Dunlap was removed from Nitec on August 30, 1976, exactly one month before the presentation of the annual accounts with an anticipated profit amounting to almost 5 million dollars. On September 30, the financial statements closed, and the first accounting problems emerged: the auditors, in charge of the financial statement certification, expressed some concerns. According to their findings, Nitec should have not recorded a profit at all, but a loss of 5.5 million dollars: the sales, apparently accounted for, were actually the result of massive falsifications and fraudulent accounting entries. Specifically, the auditors contested the presence of unrecorded expenditure, overestimation of inventory, accounting for non-existent sales, and overvaluation of (available) cash for US$201,700 dollars. In 1982 the company filed for bankruptcy and was seized by the city of Niagara Falls for the non-payment of taxes. Owing to the enormous complexity of the events, Nitec's legal battle against Dunlap was inconclusive and in 1983 the company's lawyers reported to the bankruptcy court that bringing the case to court would cost US$600,000, an amount that Nitec did not actually possess. For this reason, the court ruled a payment to Dunlap of US$50,000 to close the case.

After a few months looking for a job, in 1977 Dunlap was hired by *American Can Co.* at its headquarters in Greenwich, Connecticut. As general manager of strategic planning in two divisions, he reduced costs by closing plants, dismissing employees, reducing investments and assets. Because of these drastic cuts, profits enjoyed a big surge.

In 1982, Dunlap changed industry type completely and was hired by *Manville Corp.*, an asbestos-producing company whose headquarters was in Denver, Colorado. Here he was given the task of solving financial problems and relaunching the business. Al Dunlop's experience in this new company was very short, the owner (Johns Manville) opting for voluntary bankruptcy due to huge liabilities for asbestos injuries in the same year of Dunlap's hiring.

In 1983 Dunlap was hired by Kohlberg, Kraft, Roberts & Co. (KKR). It was an investment company, specialized in leveraged buyout operations, which in 1982 bought *Lily-Tulip Inc.* (hereafter called Lily-Tulip) paying US$180 million. Dunlap was hired by KKR to make Lily-Tulip more efficient, improving inventory control, reducing interest costs but also eliminating the production and sale of low-margin products and, more generally, trimming costs. Given these objectives, Dunlap fired most of the managers (11 out of 13) and a lot of the staff (20%), in particular those employed at headquarters, forcing in this way the reallocation of operations to other separate branches. He sold numerous old plants, increased spending on research and development of automatic equipment, and introduced a new line of products. Within 12 months, the company was able to generate income, rising from a loss of US$10.8 million in 1982 to a profit of US$8.3 million in 1983 and US$23 million in 1984, also reducing debt from US$165 to US$43 million. Dunlap also acquired the merit of having listed the company on March 14, 1984, through a public bid valued at US$45.6 million. In 1986, Dunlap left Lily-Tulip after earning US$8 million.

In 1991 Dunlap decided to move to Australia where he got a five-year contract and became CEO initially of Australian National Industries and later of Packer Consolidated Press Holdings with the precise task (by now par for the course with Dunlap) of restructuring them. The first (i.e. *Australian National Industries*) was a metalworking company burdened by financial and strategic problems caused by the excessive diversification of production and the presence of a quantity of leased equipment. Dunlap sold non-core activities, reduced the workforce (by half), and focused the company on its basic technical capabilities. The second (i.e. *Packer Consolidated Press Holdings*) was a colossus with 431 companies that in 1992 lost US$25 million. Dunlap reduced costs and increased the profits of 331 divisions. Despite the good results, after only two years his contract was closed because the owners believed that some sales of assets had been carried out below the market value. Dunlap returned to America in May 1993 with US$40 million, ready for a new turnaround experience.

Dunlap's managerial experiences outlined thus far have a number of features in common with those described in Sunbeam Corp's case (Table 3.7).

Even though some common features are present in all Dunlap's working experiences previous to that in Sunbeam Corp., the closest similarities can be observed in Dunlap's working experience immediately before taking over the reins at Sunbeam Corporation: in April 1994 Dunlap became CEO of *Scott Paper Co.* (hereafter called Scott). The financial situation of this company was deteriorating at that time: from a net income of US$401 million in 1988, Scott recorded a decline in net income of US$148 million in 1990 and a loss of US$277 million in 1993. This decline was mainly due to huge capital investments (about US$700 million between 1989 and 1990) in the S.D. Warren paper mill, economic recession in 1990, growing capacity of competitors, and fall of commodity-paper prices (Gilson 2010). Dunlap was the first external CEO of the company since its foundation. Immediately, he bought US$2 million of Scott's stock (with his own money) and reduced the executive committee from 11 to only 5 members, including 3 new appointments of people with whom Dunlap had previously worked (including Russ Kersh who would also follow him to Sunbeam Corp). His first goal in Scott Paper Corp. was to analyse all stages of the production process and develop a credible

Table 3.7 Albert Dunlap's main working experiences

Kimberly-Clark Corporation
1963—First job. Dunlap assimilated the management style of his boss Frank Nobbe.
1966—After four years of experience in Kimberly-Clark, Dunlap was hired by another company.
Sterling Pulp & Paper Co.
1966—General manager of the plant in Eau Claire (Wisconsin).
1973—Dunlap left office when the owner of the Sterling died in June 1973.
Max Phillips & Sons Inc.
1973—Three-year contract as manager. Dunlap was fired after less than two months. Dunlap sued the company that agreed to pay him US$55,000.
Nitec Paper Corporation
1974—Manager for corporate restructuring.
1976—(August 30) Dunlap was removed exactly one month before the presentation of the annual accounts with an anticipated profit amounting to almost 5 million dollars.
1976—(September 30) Auditors' concern about financial statements.
1983—Dunlap received US$50,000 to close the legal case.
American Can Co. and Manville Corp.
1977–1982—General manager at company's headquarters.
Lily-Tulip Inc.
1983—Dunlap was hired.
1984—(March 14) Public bid valued at US$45.6 million. Dunlap took the company public.
1986—Dunlap left Lily-Tulip after earning US$8 million.
Consolidated Press Holdings:
1991—Dunlap was hired to restructure the company.
He sold most of the holding company's businesses and revoked company perks.
Scott Paper Co.:
1993—Dunlap was hired to restructure the company.
1995—The company was sold to Kimberly-Clark for around US$7 billion.
Sunbeam Corp.
1996—CEO. The company was in a situation of financial distress especially because of poor performance in the early 1990s and a lost lawsuit against the former CEO, fired in 1992.
1998—An analyst from the journal *Barron's Online* was the first to focus on the improper accounting practices implemented in Sunbeam from October 1996 to June 1998. His article sparked Dunlap's resignation, stopping the fraud implementation.

---

restructuring plan to identify possible room for improvement. From this preliminary analysis, it turned out that Scott Paper Corp. was a company burdened by major operational inefficiencies. A substantial part of the costs could, in fact, be reduced by rationalizing the available resources and outsourcing part of the services. The outsourcing of some general services hitherto performed in the central office and involving some 450 people, would allow a saving of well over US$15 million (Gilson 2010). Efficiency, on the other hand, could lead to much wider and more significant margins for improvement, deriving both from a better management of the processes and from the redesign of the work. In particular, savings for a total amount of US$92 million (Gilson 2010) could be obtained by making greater use of videoconferences, reducing travel expenses, decreasing project workers, and renegotiating the prices of services offered by external companies. On the basis of this plan, Dunlap made two major moves: the first was to reduce costs by eliminating all expenses considered useless, while the other was to divest assets in order to obtain cash with which to address the burden of debt, to avoid a further credit rating downgrade. To achieve the first objective and reduce costs, Dunlap closed or sold 41 of the 60 company structures, with drastic dismissals: by the end of 1994, Dunlap had reduced the workforce by 34%, laying off about 11,000 employees among employees at headquarters (minus 71%), management (minus 50%), and hourly workers (minus 20%). In addition, donations (equal to about US$3–4 million per year) were no longer granted to non-profit associations, on the grounds that "they were not in line with the interests of the shareholders". Moreover, the new management identified the company's core business as paper products for hygiene and domestic use, and all activities not pertinent to this were discontinued, starting with S.D. Warren, the glossy paper division sold to a South African company for US$1.6 billion in December 1994. In the same vein, a power plant was sold in Mobile Alabama for US$350 million, health care and food services units for US$110 million, but also the corporate jet and the 55-acre headquarters outside Philadelphia, which were moved to Florida, in a rented 30,000-square-foot building. The proceeds from these sales were partly used to reduce the debt (US$1.5 billion) and partly invested in facilities, global expansion initiatives, and marketing campaigns. In particular, a joint venture was established with Shanghai Paper Ltd. which led to Scott Paper becoming the first paper products company to operate in China. Several investments were funded for the construction or expansion of plants, in particular in Mexico (US$148 million to expand production capacity), Owensboro (US$580 million for the purchase of a new machine), and Yucca (US$40 million for the construction of a new plant). More than 100 new products were launched, redesigning packaging and giving more importance to rebranding in Europe. The pursuit of the two objectives described above (reduction of costs and debt) involved *the reversal of the company's results* from 1994: US$209,800 million in profit at the end of 1994 against a loss of US$277,000 million in the previous year, with an increase of over 175%. The degree of solvency rating improved, as did the value of the company's stock which rose from US$38, the day that Dunlap was hired, to US$60 at the end of 1994, and then increased to US$90 in June 1995. On July 17, 1995, *the merger agreement* between Scott Paper and Kimberly-Clark became official. The incorporation, which took place at the end of the year, cost Kimberly-Clark about US$6.8 billion. After the agreement, Dunlap resigned with a pay package of US$100 million, including US$12 million in salary (paid off), US$60 million in stock options, and US$20 million for a non-compete agreement and because of the difference from the sale of his shares in Scott Paper. A generous handshake was also provided for five other managers, including Kersh and Murtagh.

After the "successful" experience in Scott, Dunlap was considered the possessor of a perfect corporate restructuring strategy that permitted companies to exit from the path of financial distress. He was reckoned "a corporate turnaround specialist" (Gilson 2010, p. 713). Dunlap also wrote a book, entitled *Mean Business: How I Save Bad Companies and Make Good Companies Great* (Dunlap and Andelman 1997), from which, obviously, Dunlap's earlier inglorious working experiences in Nitec and Max Phillips & Sons Inc. were omitted. The book focuses on *the main objective* of a company, and therefore of a corporate restructuring, that is, to "make money for the shareholders, first and foremost" (Dunlap and Andelman 1997, Chap. 14). Shareholders are, in fact, the subjects to whom all efforts must be directed because they are "the people who invest in a company, that is not the employees, not the suppliers, and not the community" (Dunlap and Andelman 1997, Chap. 13). Dunlap's prioritizing is in fact in line with the main features of the systems of corporate governance in Anglo-Saxon countries. Jones (2011) draws a distinction between two main typologies of accounting fraud that can be associated with different systems of corporate governance: an excess of power retained by entrepreneurs or managers is usually at the origin of misstatement crimes in continental (European) financial systems, whereas in the US (as in most of the Anglo-Saxon countries) accounting fraud seems mainly to result from the pressure on performance exerted by financial investors, market analysts, and internal budgeting on top and middle managers. This second typology represents the set of pertinent circumstances in our case: Dunlap's managerial conduct aimed, above all, at meeting expected results. Therefore, in order to achieve the maximization of the value of the shares, it was opportune to tie the remuneration of the executives to the value of the shares themselves: this alignment of interests makes it easier to obtain the best results (Dunlap and Andelman 1997, Chap. 12). According to Dunlap, this is possible through the four rules described in his book. They are well-enough established well enough and indeed quite common rules in the international management literature, but they take on a particular significance in Dunlap's recommended implementation. First, "get the right management team" (Dunlap and Andelman 1997, Chap. 3) is a concise rule, but revealing in the context of the fraudulent plans orchestrated by Dunlap together with a few (regular) collaborators. Kersh, Murtagh, and Don Burnett had been Dunlap's chosen henchmen since their working experience in Lily-Tulip (Table 3.8). In his book, Dunlap suggests that a company is not always able to overcome corporate financial distress with the sole input of its current management. Pre-existing managers inevitably have many personal interests involved and may therefore lack the will to act drastically. The recruitment of subjects from completely outside the company is fundamental because they will have an objective vision of its

Table 3.8 Dunlap's dream management team in his different corporate experiences

Years	Albert Dunlap	Russel A. Kersh	John Murtagh	Don Burnett
1977	Senior vice president of American Can Co.			Consultant in American Can Co.
1983	President and chief executive in Lily-Tulip Inc.	Administrative position in Lily-Tulip Inc.	Senior purchasing executive in Lily-Tulip Inc.	Consultant in Lily-Tulip Inc.
1994	Chief executive officer in Scott Paper Co.	Senior vice president (finance and administration) in Scott Paper Co.	Senior vice president and general counsel in Scott Paper Co.	Consultant in Scott Paper Co.
1996–1998	Chief executive officer in Sunbeam Corp.	Chief financial officer of Sunbeam Corp.		Consultant in Sunbeam Corp. (and partner at Coopers & Lybrand accounting firm)

corporate distressed status and will be able to make drastic decisions for the good of the business. Moreover, large boards of directors are judged to be unproductive. Too many people involved in decisions imply a considerable amount of time spent on reaching agreement. In a distressed company it is necessary to eliminate the old corporate culture to make room for a new one, more suited to the characteristics and needs of a restructured company. This is possible only if the change starts at the top and involves people with a different mentality as well as a different and better way of working. According to this principle, in every restructuring, Dunlap dismisses most of the top management, replaces it with a few trusted collaborators, and creates a slim board of directors to make quick decisions. All this boils down to a decision-making process that involves fewer people with the common goal of relaunching the company. In his book Dunlap justifies the presence of his small band of habitual—and well-paid—collaborators, saying that it is important to be assisted by the people with whom you have already worked because they will be better able to meet the demands of the situation, without asking too many details and doing things in the right way, for the good of the company and its shareholders. This objective is supported by the aforementioned economic incentives given to management and linked to share returns.

The second rule referred to in the book concerns *the reduction of costs* through redundancies, the elimination of the head office, the closure of plants, and the reduction of stock keeping units (SKUs). In fact, the first thing that Dunlap had always done in his restructuring was to dismiss most of the employees, first and foremost, those in administrative positions and employed at headquarters because "the money is made by the guy in the plant". Subsequently, Dunlap also fires workers who work in plants that are old or useless (i.e. that must be closed or sold). These interventions clearly require the reallocation of those operations still necessary to the other production facilities that remain operational. The third rule concerns the precise definition of the core business, that is, the main production activity on which the company's existence is based. It is important that management is able to identify *the core business* of its company as precisely as possible and that it is able to maintain it over time, without losing its focus. Anything that is not part of the company's deep identity must be decommissioned to allow time, effort, and money to be concentrated on the characteristic activity, the only one able to keep the company alive and competitive. For these reasons, after having defined the core business, Dunlap sells everything that does not fit in with it and invests the return in R&D and new equipment, usually to set up a new product line or to renew the production strategy. The fourth and last rule refers to *the strategic vision* that must be clear and widely communicated if one is to be able to reach it. This strategic vision requires a set of activities to restructure the distressed company quickly: these activities must be fast and targeted because the restructuring can only be rapid, as time is at a premium.

The similarities between the Scott and Sunbeam cases can be revisited in the light of these rules, discussed extensively in his book (Dunlap and Andelman 1997). First of all, Dunlap's cutbacks (firing not only workers, but especially headquarters staff and managers within a few months) were interpreted as cost-slashing and restructuring techniques, but they were motivated at least as much by the desire to work with his trusted collaborators in order to fully implement his "usual" strategies. This had to do with the mechanisms of governance internal to the company and the CEO's desire, or need, to enjoy full powers. Indeed, during his time at Scott, Dunlap fired most of the top management, reducing the executive committee from 11 to only 5 members. Of these, only two (i.e. Basil Anderson and Newt White) were Scott managers before Dunlap, while the others (i.e. Russell Kersh, John Murtaugh, and Jack Dailey) had already worked with him before his position in Scott. In Sunbeam Corp., four of the five board members were chosen by Dunlap himself (the fifth was a main shareholder, Michael Price). In particular, Russell Kersh would be accused by the SEC of having orchestrated the fraudulent scheme together with Dunlap. Indeed, during his heading up of Sunbeam, Dunlap extracted a new agreement with doubled salaries, millionaire grants of shares, and options for both himself and Kersh.

This is strictly related to the second point: Dunlap sought to align management and shareholders' interests. In this way, the maximization of the profit attributable to shareholders become the primary objective for the entire company, reinforcing the correlation between management pay and company performance. This explains why Dunlap, immediately after being hired, bought shares of both Scott Paper and Sunbeam. Moreover, generous stock option packages were granted to several executives, including Kersh and Murtagh.

Another key feature is related to the identification of the core business of the company and to the divestment of all non-core assets. Dunlap identified Scott's core business as paper products, probably because the company was a market leader in that sector and had a line of products with well-known brand-names. Consequently, everything that was not strictly pertinent (e.g. a power plant, restaurant, health care business, corporate jet, Philadelphia headquarters) was sold. The proceeds from these sales were used to reduce debt by US$1.5 billion and invested in core assets. In Sunbeam, after Dunlap's hire as CEO, 18 of the 26 plants were closed.

The similarities between Dunlap's strategies at Scott Paper Co. and Sunbeam Corp are also evident from an analysis of his fraudulent plans as reported by SEC Release No. 45653 (March 27, 2002). "Such proceedings arose from inaccurate annual financial statements filed by Kimberly-Clark with the Securities and Exchange Commission for the years ended December 31, 1995, through December 31, 1998, and quarterly financial statements from March 31, 1996, through the quarter ended March 31, 1999. These issues arose in connection with a US$1.44 billion charge for restructuring and other unusual charges that Kimberly-Clark recorded after its merger with Scott Paper Company in December 1995" (SEC 2002, p. 1). The release emphasizes the improper accounting practices implemented by Kimberly-Clark and underlines that some of them derived from accounts created because of the merger with Scott. In particular, some losses, possibly unexpected deriving from Scott, were charged by Kimberly-Clark against the restructuring reserve subaccount instead of recording them as a current-period expense as required by US GAAP. The improper accounting practices implemented in Scott are related to those applied in Kimberly-Clark. This evidence highlights the concepts of failure and fraud as paths that can derive from, and be reinforced by, those of other companies. Indeed, the same release (SEC 2002) emphasizes the improper accounting practices that were implemented before the merger concerning accounts receivable adjustments (SEC 2002, p. 4) and inventory write-down (SEC 2002, p. 5). Regarding the first (i.e. accounts receivable adjustments), before the merger of Kimberly-Clark and Scott became definitive, the acquirer discovered that Scott salesmen had offered substantial sales incentives that had not yet been processed. In order to cover the costs of these incentives, US$45 million was included as a programme in the restructuring plan as of December 31, 1995. Scott's accountants and independent auditor had assured Kimberly-Clark that the original accrual, excluding the US$45 million, was sufficient. Antitrust considerations prevented Kimberly-Clark from performing a thorough due diligence on Scott's sales practices prior to the merger. Later in 1996, Kimberly-Clark discovered that the amounts actually claimed under Scott's sales incentive schemes were US$69 million more than expected. In 1997, amounts actually claimed by customers were about US$30 million more than expected. Regarding the second improper accounting practice (i.e. inventory write-down), in 1996 Kimberly-Clark created programmes for "end-user pricing contracts" for an amount of US$55 million. They consisted of unfavourable contracts and were the result of negotiations realized before the merger by the Scott sales force at unrealistic list prices and with limited controls. Moreover, Kimberly-Clark recorded a US$13.3 million inventory write-down for excessive Scott inventory levels. The SEC release suggests, therefore, that improper accounting practices were implemented in Kimberly-Clark before its merger with Scott and when Dunlap was its CEO. For this reason, finding similarities in the accounting loopholes exploited first in Scott and then in Sunbeam takes on an additional significance. The main features of the fraudulent schemes implemented by Dunlap and his collaborators can be summarized in the following three main points that have been described above for Scott case. The first concerns losses charged against the restructuring reserve subaccount instead of recording them as a current-period expense. This fraudulent use of restructuring reserve subaccount was also practised at Sunbeam, while unrecorded expenses is a gimmick common to all the frauds implemented by Dunlap. The second regards sales incentive schemes not yet processed. This fraudulent ploy was also applied at both Nitec and Sunbeam. The third refers to inventory write-down programmes for "end-user pricing contracts", consisting in unfavourable contracts of sales at unrealistic list prices and with limited controls. This fraudulent ploy was also applied at Sunbeam.

On the one hand, the main points of Dunlap's strategy and fraudulent ploys which we have described represent relevant similarities between the cases of Scott and Sunbeam. On the other hand, such cases are different because of (at least) three features setting them apart: auditors' evaluations, types of macro-failure, and timings of fraud discovery. First, Dunlap's managerial evaluation and strategy were similar in the frauds implemented at Scott and at Sunbeam, but an important difference between them concerns auditing evaluations. On one side, Scott's independent auditor is only cited: he is not involved in fraud procedure.[8] On the other, in the case of Sunbeam, auditors' behaviour, faced with the accounting fraud, was

---

[8] "Scott's accountants and independent auditor had assured Kimberly-Clark that the original accrual, excluding the $45 million, was sufficient" (SEC 2002, d. Accounts Receivable Adjustments).

really peculiar, as described above. Phillip E. Harlow, the Arthur Andersen partner in charge of the Sunbeam audit, discovered some of the fraudulent accounting transactions and convinced Dunlap to cut US$3 million of sham profit, and the remaining part of profit was considered "immaterial". According to the agency theory, auditors (agents) used their professional knowledge, asymmetrical information, and the flexibility of auditing rules (at that time) to distract the attention of the principals (owners, shareholders, and investors) from news that would be harmful, if not catastrophic. This auditing practice has been called "creative auditing" and was implemented in the exceptional case of Sunbeam: it may represent the end point of a "blind evolutionary path" because of the impossibility of applying it in a different more stringent and regulated context (Agostini and Favero 2017). Indeed, in the Sunbeam case, the auditors' evaluation was generously attributed to a low level of scepticism, allowing the auditing firm to continue its work until Enron's scandal. Dunlap (the CEO) was (rightly) banned from similar work, but he was scapegoated alone (or only with a few collaborators) instead of also involving the auditors, punished only with a fine. Auditors would later be increasingly scapegoated themselves (Guénin-Paracini and Gendron 2010), when (in the early 2000s) further corporate scandals (originating in the 1990s) started to emerge. In that period, a number of auditors were "fined or settled out of court" (Jones 2011). This seems to be consistent with the general evolution of legislative measures against fraud over the last decades, which focus more and more on auditing failure. Based on these premises, auditing rules and accounting standards will be investigated in the following paragraphs. The second main difference between the Scott and Sunbeam cases concerns the types of macro-failure (i.e. the last stage of a firm's life cycle that represents an important type of discontinuance, requiring a radical change in the firm that wants to survive). Dunlap managed to sell Scott, while this was not possible for Sunbeam. According to the abovementioned rating of fraudsters' preferences about the types of macro-failure, Dunlap was able to apply the first-best strategy in Scott: selling the company to Kimberly-Clark, he could then depart from Scott only 20 months after his hiring with a reward of US$100 million. Dunlap thought to apply the same strategy to Sunbeam. This was a mistake because his own celebrity pushed Sunbeam stock to premium levels, making it too rich a dish for most acquirers, and a sale proved impossible (in spite of the many attested attempts). Dunlap's corporate sale strategy was profitably applied only to Scott, making him (and his mode of corporate restructuring) a sort of "miracle worker": he achieved fame by running Scott for two years, drastically pruning its operations and finally selling the company to rival Kimberley-Clark. In Scott's case, Dunlap could choose the preferable type of macro-failure: the sale of the company to Kimberley-Clark permitted him to cover up fraud under the so-called veil of acquisition. This conclusion emphasizes the importance of the role of sales and acquisitions. In the case of Sunbeam, as the sale of the company became impossible (Byrne 1999), he resorted to the second-best strategy of acquiring other companies: this represents an alternative tool for concealing accounting fraud and camouflaging overvalued company stocks. The sale of Sunbeam should have represented the final step of the process of business reorganization started by Dunlap and the realization of the value created in that process. This finding has by contrast an important implication for the ongoing research concerning accounting fraud, information uncertainty, and acquisition losses (Erickson et al. 2011; literature about disclosed and undisclosed frauds as summarized in Jones 2011). Dunlap's experience suggests that managers committing fraud look at the acquisition of other companies only as a second-best strategy: they prefer their companies to be acquired by other companies because this would almost certainly conceal successfully the fraudulent accounting behaviour preceding the acquisition. The financial statements of acquired companies could well be an interesting source for empirical investigation of the diffusion of undisclosed fraud. In the Scott case, the merger agreement with Kimberley-Clark became official in July 1995 and fraudulent ploys were partially disclosed after seven years (SEC 2002), by then subsequent to the disclosure of Sunbeam fraud in 1998. This represents the third (and last) main difference between Scott and Sunbeam: the timing of fraud discovery. On the one hand, in the Scott case, the fraud remains substantially undisclosed because the SEC (2002) only accused Kimberley-Clark of fraudulent ploys many years after the acquisition of Scott. On the other hand, in the Sunbeam case the fraud was discovered promptly and in a peculiar way: the attention of an analyst from the journal *Barron's Online* was caught by the steep decrease of Sunbeam's stock. He was the first (in 1998) to focus on the improper accounting practices implemented in Sunbeam from October 1996 to June 1998. His article led to Dunlap's resignation, terminating the fraud. Jerry Levin, who succeeded Dunlap in Sunbeam, claimed to be shocked: "I find it most unusual that anyone could be hired as a chief executive of a major company without having their background thoroughly checked" (Norris 2001b). Indeed, neither Sunbeam nor the

SEC were aware of the earlier unsuccessful experiences in Nitec and Max Phillips & Sons Inc. Such information would, to say the least, have been relevant: Dunlap was fired after less than two months in Max Phillips & Sons Inc. for neglecting his duties and speaking disparagingly of the company's head. He then sued the company which had to agree to pay him US$55,000 (i.e. US$10,000 for the violation of the signed three-year contract, US$30,000 for unspecified personal injury, and US$15,000 for reputational damage). He was also removed from Nitec in order to not prejudice the image of the company, and more especially because of the internal personal relationships with managers. Moreover, immediately after his dismissal, the auditors Arthur Young, conducting their certification of statements, declined to give an unqualified opinion. According to their findings, Nitec should have not recorded a profit, but a loss of US$5.5 million because most of its claimed sales were the result of massive falsifications and fraudulent accounting entries. Specifically, the auditors contested the presence of unrecorded expenses, the overestimation of the inventory, the accounting of non-existent sales, and the overvaluation of cash for US$201,700. In doing this, Dunlap did not act alone but was helped by the financial vice president Albert J. Edwards, who became, after the discovery of the fraud, himself the key witness against the CEO. Edwards later testified that the accounting books were falsified under the orders of Dunlap, who sometimes specified in detail which accounting items to falsify, while at other times he indicated only by how much the profits should increase compared to the previous month, leaving him with the task of deciding operationally how to make this apparent. Clearly, such directives to Edwards were all purely oral. In 1982, Nitec filed for bankruptcy and was seized by the city of Niagara Falls for the non-payment of taxes. Due to the enormous complexity of the events in dispute, Nitec's legal battles against Dunlap were inconclusive. For this reason, in 1983 the company accepted the payment to Dunlap of US$50,000 to close the case. Dunlap has omitted both these experiences in his book and in his own curriculum for obvious reasons. Moreover, in spite of these legal vicissitudes between himself and both these companies (Nitec and Max Phillips & Sons Inc.), neither Sunbeam nor the SEC were aware of them. Dunlap was thus able to become CEO of Scott and Sunbeam with the consequences we have described. This highlights the lack of legislative measures against fraud at that time. The next paragraph will focus on the evolution of both laws and standards after the high season of accounting scandals in 2001.

Summarizing, the beginning of this paragraph focused on the timeliness of auditors' going concern decisions by considering the time of their issuance during corporate paths of severe financial distress. It appears to sustain the investors' complaint: although going concern assessment has for years been American auditors' responsibility, after the season of accounting scandals in 2001, investors have complained that, by the time auditors make the assessment, American businesses may be on the verge of bankruptcy or a delisting from their stock exchange. Concerning auditors' competence, previous research has confirmed that auditors have the ability to identify a company with going concern problems, but some empirical studies have shown that many companies in the year prior to bankruptcy receive an audit report in which no going concern uncertainty is disclosed. So, the main problem seems to be the timeliness of American auditors' going concern assessments. For this reason, the implemented analysis verifies the abovementioned investors' complaint about American auditors' timeliness in going concern assessment. The sample analysed considers all the US fraud cases and the matched no-tort cases included in UCLA–LoPucki Bankruptcy Research Database, acting in a division different from the H. A survival time analysis highlights the timing of auditors' going concern decision. In order to test the hypotheses, the implemented analysis considers the year of the last unqualified report and the date of final bankruptcy. The results of the analysis suggest that going concern doubts and bankruptcy often overlap because an entity receiving a going concern opinion may be on the verge of filing for bankruptcy, and so very close to macro-failure. After this initial investigation through descriptive statistics and survival time functions, the analysis enables us to gather some details about the turnover of auditors. Five examined cases changed the auditing firm during the analysed corporate financial paths (between the relevant micro-failure and the macro-failure): such changes occurred three years before the macro-failure in three cases, two years before the macro-failure only in one case, and one year before the macro-failure again only in a single case. Moreover, an outlier emerges from the implemented time analysis: Sunbeam's path of severe financial distress is longer than the usual path after the disclosure of the fraud. The historical micro-analysis (Agostini and Favero 2017) emphasizes the main reasons of the emergence of this outlier. In particular, the CEO of the company (Dunlap) is considered the main orchestrator of Sunbeam's fraud, which presents peculiar features. Similarities in the management strategy and exploitation of accounting loopholes are identified also in Dunlap's working experiences before Sunbeam, especially when he was CEO of Scott. The analysis permits us to identify and explain some common traits and differences between disclosed and undisclosed frauds of distressed companies. Such explanation of corporate financial distress aims to answer a request advanced by authoritative studies (Cybinski 2001; Humphrey 2008; Lee 2004; Parker 2005) concerning the need for detailed qualitative contextual research of famous corporate scandals. In particular, Parker (2012, p. 67) observes: "The qualitative agenda has much to offer in unpacking these processes of accounting, auditing and accountability, and in addition translating qualitative management accounting issues and research designs into the financial accounting and auditing arenas, as well as bringing questions of internal management and accounting control systems in large scale corporate crash experiences under the microscope." The analysis of Dunlap's strategies and loopholes in different distressed companies suggests that companies committing fraud view the acquisition of other companies only as a second-best strategy. They prefer to be acquired, as selling seems to provide a more successful cover-up of previous fraudulent accounting than acquisition. Thus, the historical financial statements of acquired companies may be a rich source for the investigation of possible undisclosed frauds. Our detailed study of Sunbeam also highlights the need for the further development of both accounting and auditing regulation, as illustrated in the next paragraph.

3.4   New Standards, Liquidation Basis, and Concluding Remarks

The auditors' evaluation in the case of Sunbeam just reviewed was attributed to a practice known as "creative auditing" (Agostini and Favero 2017) that was made possible by the legislative framework at that time. A series of US scandals (of which Enron is the most famous) prejudiced the capital markets, especially in the last 20 years, and gave rise to an interest in preventing economic disasters. American regulators issued the Sarbanes–Oxley Act (hereafter called SOX) in 2002, aiming to limit or even eliminate fraudulent ploys in financial statements, laying down both management's and auditors' responsibilities regarding financial statements. These changes in SEC rules and regulations in accordance with SOX became effective after November 15, 2004. With respect to management's responsibility, Section 404 of SOX requires that entities' managements, and certifications prepared by specific corporate officers, report on the effectiveness of internal controls and material weaknesses in financial statements. In particular, Section 302 of SOX requires an issuer's principal executive officers and principal financial officers to certify each report, including transitional ones, filed or submitted by the issuer (Kwak et al. 2009). After the evaluation of internal controls, the certifying officers should acknowledge any significant change and evaluate substantial consequences in internal controls, including any corrective action with regard to significant deficiencies or material weaknesses. Management's responsibility is then completed by that of the auditors, who are charged to report on client's assertions. Indeed, after the scandals season in 2001, auditors' responsibility has been reinforced in three ways in the US context: the described SOX, a new auditing standard (SAS No. 99 "Consideration of Fraud in a Financial Statement Audit") concerning fraud consideration, and the revision of the abovementioned SAS No. 59 concerning going concern evaluation. The first legislative measure (SOX) reinforced both management's and auditors' responsibilities: it is considered the strongest regulation passed since the 1930s (Klass 2003). The second is the issuance of SAS No. 99 ("Consideration of Fraud in a Financial Statement Audit")[9] that recommends the following to auditors: meaningful risk assessment procedures, professional scepticism in gathering and evaluating audit evidence, brainstorming sessions to discuss the risks of material misstatements due to fraud, and forensic audit training. The third is the revision of SAS No. 59 ("The Auditor's Consideration of an Entity's Ability to Continue as a Going Concern"). Following its issuance and until the abovementioned scandals season in 2001, SAS No. 59 was considered a guarantee for investors. Between 2001 and 2002, however, 12 out of 20 companies went bankrupt even when they had recently received an "unqualified opinion" by auditors (Venuti 2004). Because of such events, doubts arose about the validity of such auditing standards, mainly for two reasons. First, the language used by the accounting standard was considered ambiguous (Ehoff Jr and Gray 2014): in particular, some terms allowed auditors a

---

[9] SAS No. 99 replaced SAS No. 82 ("Consideration of Fraud in a Financial Statement Audit") that was issued in February 1997. This previous auditing standard was the first to mention "fraud" in its title. According to SAS No. 82, fraud could be of two types: intentional falsification of financial statements and theft of assets. For both of them, a list of risk factors should have favoured auditors' detection and assessment of fraud. In spite of this attempt to specify auditing procedure against fraud, SAS No. 82 did not increase auditors' responsibility to detect fraud beyond the key concepts of materiality and reasonable assurance (Mancino 1997).

wide latitude of interpretation. Some examples are the following: "for a reasonable period of time" and "appropriate evidential matter" (SAS 59, par. 2). Second, auditors are considered chiefly responsible for the evaluation of substantial doubt about a firm's capability to continue its activity as a going concern. Moreover, they were required to evaluate management's plans in order to alleviate the going concern issue. The standard did not impute the responsibility for predicting future conditions and events to auditors, but to the management, which was not, however, responsible for the going concern assumption. So, neither auditors nor management were considered fully responsible for the going concern issue. These factors were also strictly related to the auditors' risks recalled in the previous chapter (paragraph 2.4): risk of litigation, risk of loss of reputation, and risk of client loss may have led to auditors' hesitation in promptly taking the proper decisions about going concern especially, because of the so-called opinion shopping (Ehoff Jr and Gray 2014) that may have resulted in a sort of trade-off between audit and accounting quality. Moreover, the audit quality was not easily measurable because the grade of assurance transferred from auditors to external stakeholders (such as shareholders) could not be examined. The outcome of the audit process (i.e. going concern opinions and financial reporting quality) represented the only way to verify the audit quality. The auditors' instrument of communication was the audit opinion that should have also provided information about the audit process itself. It was influenced by the auditor's evaluation of whether there was substantial doubt about the capability of firms to continue the activity as a going concern. Managers obviously preferred an audit opinion clean of going concern doubts which would have proved costly. Under pressure from managers, auditors may have modified their audit opinion, damaging the independence of their assessment and the audit quality. When auditors failed to report that a business was not a going concern, they gave a misleading opinion, which was considered evidence of poor audit quality (Kaplan and Williams 2012). This point is especially relevant for auditors' responsibility in so far as they have traditionally been scapegoated (Girard 1972; Girard 2005; Guénin-Paracini and Gendron 2010; Jones 2011). In the US, going concern assessment has for many years been the auditor's responsibility (AICPA Statement on Auditing Standards No. 1, *Codification of Auditing Standards and Procedures*, Section 341, "The Auditor's Consideration of an Entity's Ability to Continue as a Going Concern"), but investors have recently complained that by the time auditors make the assessment, a failing business may already be on the verge of bankruptcy or a delisting from its stock exchange. This concerns the so-called expectation gap, which is the difference between the auditors' actual performance and public expectations of their responsibility (Albrecht and Willingham 1993). The complaint has been empirically analysed in the previous paragraph. US interested parties have therefore expressed a need for accounting literature that clarifies that an entity has the primary responsibility for assessing its own ability to continue as a going concern. Moreover, the financial crisis of 2008 highlighted the shortcomings of risk assessment at the micro level. Lenders and other investors in the corporate sector, along with regulators, require timely information on the default risk probability of corporates (Tinoco and Wilson 2013). This has led to the revision of the US auditing standard about the going concern evaluation. The redraft of SAS No. 59 was included, as mentioned, in the project of ASB's SAS Clarity Project. SAS No. 126 was issued to apply the clarity drafting conventions to SAS No. 59 without changing the title, but modifying the content. Thus, SAS No. 126 superseded SAS No. 59: in short, AICPA clarified the going concern issue with SAS No. 126, which was issued in June 2012 by the ASB (Accounting Standard Board, hereafter called ASB) and became effective on December 15, 2012. At that time, the FASB did not assign the responsibility for the evaluation of the substantial doubt to the management. Recalling investors' complaints, US constituents expressed a need for accounting literature to clarify that an entity (effectively its management) has the primary responsibility for assessing its ability to continue as a going concern. The FASB has agreed that accounting guidance related to the going concern assumption should be directed specifically to entities because it is the entity that is responsible for preparing its financial statements and evaluating its ability to continue as a going concern. Accordingly, the FASB concluded that guidance related to the going concern assumption should reside in the accounting literature and decided to undertake a specific project to determine what analysis and disclosures in financial statements management should be required when there is substantial doubt about an entity's ability to continue as a going concern. The accounting project called "The Liquidation Basis of Accounting and Going Concern (Formerly Disclosures about Risks and Uncertainties)" was divided into two phases. The objective of the first phase was to provide guidance on how and when an entity should apply the liquidation basis of accounting. The objectives of the second phase were providing guidance on both whether and how an entity should judge its ability to continue as a going concern and, if so, the nature and extent of any disclosure requirements to that effect. The initial objective, then, of the project about going concern was to emphasize management responsibility in a matter (i.e. going concern) which has traditionally been the province of auditors because of the peculiarity of American going concern rules: in this sense, the project aimed also to bring about a convergence with the international standards. In fact, on the one hand, the International Accounting Standards Board (IASB) Framework makes two underlying assumptions: first, that financial statements are prepared on the accrual basis and, second, that the reporting entity is normally a going concern. On the other hand, FASB Concepts Statements extensively discussed the need for accrual accounting procedures, but only briefly discussed going concern and did not identify either as underlying assumptions. From the beginning of this convergence process between the two standard setters, it seemed clear that ironing out standards' difference about going concern assumptions would be challenging. This has resulted in the project's rather peculiar evolution: the FASB new statement objectives and developing path were revised, and in a radical way, several times. This was related to the difference between accounting and auditing standards that has been especially relevant for the management going concern assessment: the FASB project overlapped with rules and standards of other American agencies (e.g. SEC, AICPA, PCAOB). In the end, the FASB met the requirements of the second phase of the project issuing the following: a going concern Exposure Draft in 2008; a proposed accounting standards update (entitled "Presentation of Financial Statements (Topic 205) Disclosure of Uncertainties About an Entity's Going Concern Presumption") in 2013; a new accounting standard (entitled "Presentation of Financial Statements, Going Concern (Subtopic 205-40) Disclosure of Uncertainties About an Entity's Ability to Continue as a Going Concern") in 2014. This new accounting standard incorporates and (partially) revises some principles already adopted into auditing standards. Firstly, the new accounting standard requires an annual *and* interim evaluation of the reporting period where audits were generally carried out annually (auditing standards had not considered the interim period). Secondly, it defines "substantial doubt" while auditing standards did not; this definition is principally based on likelihood. Thirdly, it sets a look-forward period of one year from the financial statement issuance date in place of the shorter look-forward period of one year from the balance sheet date envisaged by the auditing standards. In the new accounting principle, a flowchart (Fig. 3.4) "depicts the decision process to follow for evaluating whether there is substantial doubt about an entity's ability to continue as a going

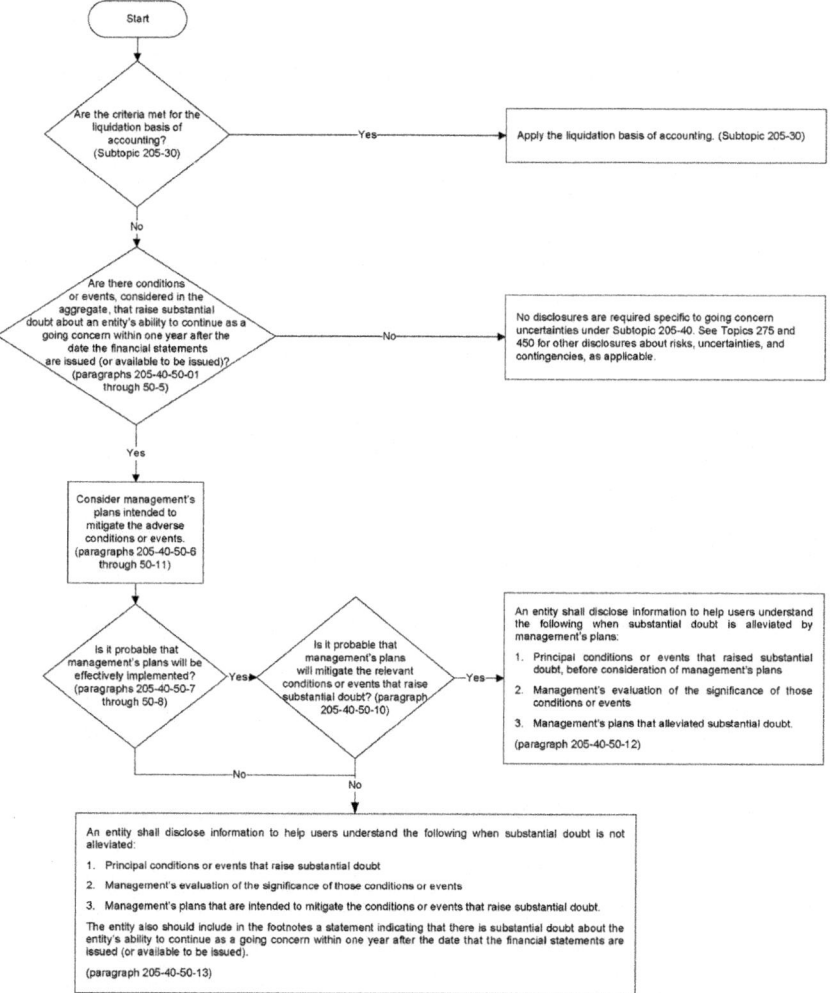

Fig. 3.4 Decision process to follow for evaluating whether there is substantial doubt about an entity's ability to continue as a going concern and determining related disclosure requirements according to US generally accepted accounting principles (Presentation of Financial Statements—Going Concern, Subtopic 205-40)

concern and determining related disclosure requirements" (Presentation of Financial Statements—Going Concern, Subtopic 205-40).

After the 2014 FASB's issuance of the Accounting Standards Update No. 2014-15 (entitled "Presentation of Financial Statements—Going Concern (Subtopic 205-40): Disclosure of Uncertainties About an Entity's Ability to Continue as a Going Concern" and establishing the management's responsibility for evaluating substantial doubt and providing adequate disclosure in the footnotes), in January 2015 the ASB issued four auditing interpretations concerning SAS No. 126 (AU-C Section 570). The four interpretations included in AU-C-Section 9570 aimed to provide interpretative guidance about some of the newly introduced material in the accounting standards and concerned the following (four) matters. The first regarded the definition of substantial doubt about an entity's ability to continue as a going concern: where the entity was required to adopt the FASB accounting standards, the definition of substantial doubt to which auditors should refer was the one set out in FASB ASC 205-40. The same interpretation was applied to the second issue about the definition of the "reasonable period of time". The management had to evaluate the substantial doubt for a period longer than one year from the date of the financial statements. The auditors' assessment of the management's going concern evaluation had to be of the same period required by the financial reporting framework adopted. Thirdly, AU-C Section 9570 specified auditors' responsibilities on the requirements laid down by FASB ASC 205-40 concerning the interim financial information (AU-C Section 930, entitled "Interim Financial Information"). Substantially, if auditors identified possible inabilities to continue as a going concern during the interim reporting period, they should question the management about its plans to combat the adverse effects of the conditions and events and evaluate if the disclosure provided in the interim financial information is adequate. In addition, auditors were required to perform interim review procedures concerning the management's evaluation of the firms' capability to continue its activity as a going concern. The fourth and last interpretation provided by AU-C Section 9570, regarding Section 570 of SAS No. 126, concerned the financial statement effects when the auditor concluded there was substantial doubt or when concern about substantial doubt was alleviated through the feasibility of management's plans. The interpretation from AICPA explained that the auditor had to follow requirements by the financial reporting framework being adopted (AU-C Section 570, par. 12–13).

In 2016, in order to fully converge with the abovementioned new FASB accounting standard, AICPA issued an Exposure Draft, aiming to replace SAS No. 126. The objective was to write a standard which could be applied to different financial statements following different frameworks, which was why AICPA tried to be as neutral as possible, although, in some cases, terminology referred to FASB standards (e.g. substantial doubt). In February 2017, ASB issued the new standard SAS No. 132, entitled "The Auditor's Consideration of an Entity's Ability to Continue as a Going Concern", effective for audits of financial statements for periods ending on or after December 15, 2017, and for the interim period starting after fiscal years ending on or after December 15, 2017 (AICPA, par. 9). The six significant changes, introduced by SAS No. 132, are the following. First (i.e. auditor's objectives and related conclusions), the new standard requires the auditor to conclude separately about the appropriateness of management's use of the going concern basis of accounting. In the case of substantial doubt about a firm's capability to continue the activity as a going concern, the auditor should base his or her conclusion on audit evidence. Second (i.e. financial support by third parties or the entity's owner-manager), the auditor should obtain sufficient appropriate audit evidence regarding both the intent of the third parties to provide financing for the entity and their ability to provide the support. The intent of supporting parties may be either in the form of a written commitment obtained from the management or a direct confirmation by the supporting parties. In order to verify the ability of the supporting parties, auditors should consider the evidence of past support, solvency, and the capacity to provide financing in a timely way for the entity to meet its obligations. Third (i.e. period beyond management's assessment), auditors have to question the management about its knowledge of conditions or events beyond the period of management's evaluation. The inquiries should be aimed at understanding if other disclosure requirements are needed and judging the fairness of the presentation of the financial statements. Fourth (i.e. use of emphasis paragraph when substantial doubt is alleviated), the standard includes application material where an auditor is willing to highlight liquidity issues related to management disclosures when substantial doubt is alleviated by management's plans. Fifth (i.e. interim financial information), auditors are required to make inquiries and verify the disclosure where conditions or events could lead to the existence of substantial doubt in the period before the financial statements. Moreover, auditors may opt to include an emphasis-of-matter paragraph in the review report when they become aware of events during the review procedures on the current-period interim financial information. Sixth (i.e. special-purpose framework), it is necessary to distinguish the issues of going concern basis of accounting from the existence of substantial doubt. If the former are not relevant, the auditor is not required to obtain sufficient appropriate audit evidence concerning the appropriateness of management's use of the going concern basis of accounting. However, irrespective of whether the going concern basis of accounting is relevant, the auditor is asked to conclude, based on the evidence obtained, whether substantial doubt exists and evaluate the possible financial statement effects.

After considering US management's and auditors' responsibilities, it is also important to emphasize what happens in the case of a negative going concern evaluation. If the company cannot continue as a going concern, then its financial statements should be evaluated according to the liquidation basis of accounting. Therefore, when the liquidation becomes imminent, financial statements should no longer be prepared under the going concern basis of accounting, but rather under the liquidation basis of accounting in accordance with ASC 205-30 ("Presentation of Financial Statements—Liquidation"). Its update represents the conclusion of the first phase of the FASB project ("Liquidation Basis of Accounting and Going Concern—Formerly Disclosures About Risk and Uncertainties"). In 2013 the FASB issued the amendments "Presentation of Financial Statements (Topic 205): The Liquidation Basis of Accounting" aiming to provide guidance on when an entity should apply the liquidation basis of accounting and to provide principles for the measurement of assets and liabilities under the liquidation basis of accounting as well as any related disclosures requirement. The definition of "liquidation" added in this update standard is the following: "the process by which an entity converts its assets to cash or other assets and settles its obligations with creditors in anticipation of the entity ceasing all activities. Upon cessation of the entity's activities, any remaining cash or other assets are distributed to the entity's investors or other claimants (albeit sometimes indirectly). Liquidation may be compulsory or voluntary. Dissolution of an entity as a result of that entity being acquired by another entity or merged into another entity in its entirety and with the expectation of continuing its business does not qualify as liquidation" (ASU No. 2013-07, "Presentation of Financial Statements (Topic 205): Liquidation Basis of Accounting"). As outlined in the definition, it will be applied in case of imminent (both compulsory and voluntary) liquidation. The FASB defined liquidation as imminent in two cases. The first occurs when a plan has to be approved by the person or persons authorized to make the plan effective and it is improbable that other parties will block the execution of such plan. The second regards the case in which the plan for liquidation has been imposed by other forces (e.g. involuntary bankruptcy) and the probability that the entity will subsequently return from liquidation is remote. If a plan for liquidation was already specified in the entity's governing documents at the entity's inception, and the management operation's decisions are limited to merely carrying out the plan for liquidation, the Liquidation Basis of Accounting cannot be adopted. An example is the "limited-life entity" where a firm has been created to complete a specific project. The scope of this accounting standard is to provide a more relevant financial statement representative of the entity. For the preparation of the financial statement, the entity in liquidation must adopt a basis of accounting able to adequately inform its users about how much the organization will have available for distribution to investors after disposing of its assets and setting its obligations. Consequently, assets and liabilities are presented at net realizable value (NRV) and net settlement value (NSV), respectively. The NRV can be identified as the expected selling price less the selling costs (i.e. completion and disposal). In the estimations of selling prices finder's fees should also be considered since liquidation often requires intermediaries for the transactional activities such as agency fees or brokerage fees. Instead, the NSV is a value that needs specialist liquidation professionals to be adequately estimated. However, these values are simple estimations since no standard market values for specialized equipment exist. The entity is also required to separately indicate the costs that it expects to incur as well as income that it expects to earn during the expected period of liquidation in addition to costs for the disposal of assets and settlement of liabilities. Moreover, at the end of each reporting period of a liquidating company, estimated values should be updated if more information is available for a better estimation.

Summarizing, this paragraph emphasizes the evolution of both legislative measures and auditing standards after the series of accounting scandals in 2001. In particular the SOX (issued in 2002) aims to upgrade both management's and auditors' responsibilities in respect of financial statements. In addition, US auditing standards have evolved: after the initial redraft of SAS No. 59, SAS No. 126 superseded SAS No. 59 (in 2012) and was finally superseded by SAS No. 132 (in 2017). This last evolution was required because of a full convergence with the new accounting standard entitled "Presentation of Financial Statements, Going Concern (Subtopic 205-40) Disclosure of Uncertainties About an Entity's Ability to Continue as a Going Concern" (issued in 2014). This standard provides a definition of "substantial doubt", sets a look-forward period of one year from the financial statement issuance date, and depicts the decision process to follow for evaluating whether there is substantial doubt about an entity's ability to continue as a going concern, and determining related disclosure requirements. This is the outcome of an accounting project (entitled "The Liquidation Basis of Accounting and Going Concern—Formerly Disclosures About Risks and Uncertainties") that had a troubled gestation (the going concern Exposure Draft was issued in 2008, the final standard only in 2014) especially because of US auditors' influence and traditional primary concern with going concern judgement, as shown by the letters of comments of the 2008 Exposure Draft. Indeed, before the project, the FASB's Concepts Statements briefly discussed going concern and did not identify it as an underlying assumption (as it was in IASB Framework). These difficulties were evident also in the gradual process of convergence between the IASB and the FASB about going concern assumptions that is investigated in the next chapter.

BIBLIOGRAPHY

Agostini, M. (2013). Two common steps in firms' failing path. *Risk Governance & Control: Financial Markets & Institutions, 3*(1), 115–128.

Agostini, M., & Favero, G. (2017). Accounting fraud, business failure and creative auditing: A microanalysis of the strange case of the Sunbeam Corporation. *Accounting History, 22*(4), 472–487.

Albrecht, W. S., & Willingham, J. J. (1993). An evaluation of SAS no. 53, the auditor's responsibility to detect and report errors and irregularities. *The expectation gap standards, proceedings of the expectation gap roundtable*, 11–12.

Angeloni, S. (2016). Cautiousness on convergence of accounting standards across countries. *Corporate Communications: An International Journal, 21*(2), 246–267.

Asare, S. K. (1990). The auditor's going concern decision: A review and implications for future research. *Journal of Accounting Literature, 9*(1), 39–64.

Beaver, W. H., McNichols, M. F., & Rhie, J. W. (2005). Have financial statements become less informative? Evidence from the ability of financial ratios to predict bankruptcy. *Review of Accounting studies, 10*(1), 93–122.

Boyatzis, R. E. (1998). *Transforming qualitative information: Thematic analysis and code development.* Cleveland: Sage.

Bradford, W. C. (2014). Because that's where the money is: A theory of corporate legal compliance. *Journal of Business, Entrepreneurship & the Law, 8*, 337.

Byrne, J. A. (1999). *Chainsaw: The notorious career of Al Dunlap in the era of profit-at-any-price.* New York, NY: Harper Business.

Cybinski, P. (2001). Description, explanation, prediction—The evolution of bankruptcy studies? *Managerial Finance, 27*(4), 29–44.

DeAngelo, L. E. (1981). Auditor size and audit quality. *Journal of Accounting and Economics, 3*(3), 183–199.

Donovan, J., Frankel, R. M., & Martin, X. (2015). Accounting conservatism and creditor recovery rate. *The Accounting Review, 90*(6), 2267–2303.

Dunlap, A. J., & Andelman, B. (1997). *Mean business: How I save bad companies and make good companies great.* Simon and Schuster.

Ehoff, C., Jr., & Gray, D. (2014). Going concern: Where is it going? *Journal of Business & Economics Research, 12*(2), 121.

Erickson, M., Heitzman, S., & Zhang, X. F. (2011). Accounting fraud and the market for corporate control. *University of Chicago, Booth School of Business working paper.* Retrieved October 6, 2017, from http://www.aaifm.org/Archive/Accounting%20Fraud.pdf

Financial Accounting Standards Board (FASB). (2014). Presentation of financial statements—Going concern (Subtopic 205-40): Disclosure of uncertainties about an entity's ability to continue as a going concern. *Accounting Standards Update (ASU) No. 2014–15.* Norwalk, CT: Author.

Gilson, S. C. (2010). *Creating value through corporate restructuring: Case studies in bankruptcies, buyouts, and breakups* (Vol. 544). John Wiley & Sons.

Girard, R. (1972). *La violence et le sacré.* Grasset.

Girard, R. (2005). *Violence and the Sacred.* Baltimore, MD: Johns Hopkins University Press.

Guénin-Paracini, H., & Gendron, Y. (2010). Auditors as modern pharmakoi: Legitimacy paradoxes and the production of economic order. *Critical Perspectives on Accounting, 21*(2), 134–158.

Hail, L., Leuz, C., & Wysocki, P. (2010). Global accounting convergence and the potential adoption of IFRS by the US (Part I): Conceptual underpinnings and economic analysis. *Accounting Horizons, 24*(3), 355–394.

Holsti, O. R. (1969). *Content analysis for the social sciences and humanities.* Reading, MA: Addison-Wesley.

Humphrey, C. (2008). Auditing research: a review across the disciplinary divide. *Accounting, Auditing & Accountability Journal, 21*(2), 170–203.

Jennings, M. M., Recker, P. M., & Kneer, D. C. (1984). A source of insecurity: A discussion and an empirical examination of standards of disclosure and levels of materiality in financial statements. *Journal of Corporation Law, 10*(3), 639.

Jones, M. (Ed.). (2011). *Creative accounting, fraud and international accounting scandals*. Chichester: John Wiley & Sons.

Jones, M. J., & Shoemaker, P. A. (1994). Accounting narratives: A review of empirical studies of content and readability. *Journal of Accounting Literature, 13*, 142.

Kaplan, S. E., & Williams, D. D. (2012). Do going concern audit reports protect auditors from litigation? A simultaneous equations approach. *The Accounting Review, 88*(1), 199–232.

Klass, K. M. (2003). Left in the dark: Sarbanes-Oxley and corporate abuse of 401 (k) plan blackout periods. *The Journal of Corporation Law, 29*(4), 801–817.

Krippendorff, K. (1980). *Reliability*. John Wiley & Sons.

Krishnan, J., & Krishnan, J. (1996). The role of economic trade-offs in the audit opinion decision: An empirical analysis. *Journal of Accounting, Auditing & Finance, 11*(4), 565–586.

Kwak, W., Eldridge, S., Shi, Y., & Kou, G. (2009). Predicting material weaknesses in internal control systems after the Sarbanes-Oxley Act using multiple criteria linear programming and other data mining approaches. *Journal of Applied Business Research, 25*(6), 105.

Langevoort, D. C. (2002). Monitoring: The behavorial economics of corporate compliance with law. *Columbia Business Law Review*, 71.

Lee, T. A. (2004). Accounting and auditing research in the United States. In C. Humphrey & B. Lee (Eds.), *The real life guide to accounting research: A behind-the-scenes view of using qualitative research methods* (pp. 57–71). Amsterdam: Elsevier.

Levitan, A. S., & Knoblett, J. A. (1985). Indicators of exceptions to the going concern assumption. *Auditing-A Journal of Practice & Theory, 5*(1), 26–39.

Mancino, J. (1997). The auditor and fraud. *Journal of Accountancy, 183*(4), 32–36.

Mirza, A. A., & Ankarath, N. (2012). *Wiley International trends in financial reporting under IFRS: Including comparisons with US GAAP, China GAAP, and India accounting standards*. John Wiley & Sons.

Mutchler, J. F. (1985). A multivariate analysis of the auditor's going-concern opinion decision. *Journal of Accounting Research, 23*, 668–682.

Norris, F. (2001a, May 18). They noticed the fraud but figured it was not important. *The New York Times*.

Norris, F. (2001b, July 16). The incomplete résumé: A special report. An executive's missing years: Papering over past problems. *The New York Times*.

Parker, L. D. (2005). Corporate governance crisis down under: post-Enron accounting education and research inertia. *European Accounting Review, 14*(2), 383–394.

Parker, L. D. (2012). Qualitative management accounting research: Assessing deliverables and relevance. *Critical Perspectives on Accounting, 23*(1), 54–70.

Perkins, S., & Wylie, D. (1999). Albert Dunlap and corporate transformations (A). *Case BAB032, Babson College*. Boston: Harvard Business School Publishing.

Platt, H. D., & Platt, M. B. (2002). Predicting corporate financial distress: reflections on choice-based sample bias. *Journal of Economics and Finance, 26*(2), 184–199.

Sarbanes, P. (2002, July). Sarbanes-oxley act (SOX) of 2002. In *The public company accounting reform and investor protection act*. Washington, DC: US Congress.

Securities and Exchange Commission (SEC) Release No. 7976. May 15, 2001. *In the matter of Sunbeam Corporation*. Retrieved October 6, 2017, from https://www.sec.gov/litigation/admin/33-7976.htm

Securities and Exchange Commission (SEC) Release No. 45653. May 27, 2002. *In the matter of Kimberly-Clark Corporation and John W. Donehower*. Retrieved October 6, 2017, from https://www.sec.gov/litigation/admin/34-45653.htm

Shamrock, S. E. (2012). *IFRS and US GAAP: A comprehensive comparison* (Vol. 7). John Wiley & Sons.

Statement on Auditing Standards (SAS) No. 34. (AICPA, 1981). *The Auditor's considerations when question arises about an entity's continued existence*.

Statement on Auditing Standards (SAS) No. 54. (AICPA, 1989). *Illegal acts by clients* (AU Section 317).

Statement on Auditing Standards (SAS) No. 59. (AICPA, 1989). *The Auditor's consideration of an entity's ability to continue as a going concern*.

Statement on Auditing Standards (SAS) No. 82. (AICPA, 1997). *Consideration of fraud in a financial statement audit*.

Statement on Auditing Standards (SAS) No. 99. (AICPA, 2002). *Consideration of fraud in a financial statement audit*.

Statement on Auditing Standards (SAS) No. 126. (AICPA, 2012). *The Auditor's consideration of an entity's ability to continue as a going concern*.

Statement on Auditing Standards (SAS) No. 132. (AICPA, 2017). *The Auditor's consideration of an entity's ability to continue as a going concern*.

Sun, J., & Li, H. (2011). Dynamic financial distress prediction using instance selection for the disposal of concept drift. *Expert Systems with Applications, 38*(3), 2566–2576.

Taffler, R. J. (1982). Forecasting company failure in the UK using discriminant analysis and financial ratio data. *Journal of the Royal Statistical Society: Series A (General), 145*, 342–358.

Tinoco, M. H., & Wilson, N. (2013). Financial distress and bankruptcy prediction among listed companies using accounting, market and macroeconomic variables. *International Review of Financial Analysis, 30*, 394–419.

Venuti, E. K. (2004). The going-concern assumption revisited: Assessing a company's future viability. *The CPA Journal, 74*(5), 40.

Watts, R. L., & Zimmerman, J. L. (1983). Agency problems, auditing, and the theory of the firm: Some evidence. *The Journal of Law and Economics, 26*(3), 613–633.

Weber, P. (1985). *Content analysis: Quantitative applications in the social sciences.* Beverly Hills, CA: Sage.

Zhang, J. (2008). The contracting benefits of accounting conservatism to lenders and borrowers. *Journal of Accounting and Economics, 45*(1), 27–54.

CHAPTER 4

The International Accounting Convergence Promoted by IASB and FASB Regarding Going Concern Status

Abstract The International Accounting Standards Board's (IASB's) Framework introduced the "going concern assumption" in 1989 (IASB Framework, Paragraph 23). Today, the first International Accounting Standard (IAS 1, par. 25), turning the going concern framework idea into a requirement, specifies the going concern assumption (IAS 1, par. 25) and precisely identifies the managers' role (IAS 1, par. 26): management should take into account all available information and consider specific factors (current and expected profitability; debt repayment schedules, including replacement financing; etc.). Starting from the consideration of the international context, this chapter compares the current going concern assumptions as stated by the two sets of standards (International Financial Reporting Standards (IFRS) and US Generally Accepted Accounting Principles (GAAP)) after the issuance of the new US accounting standard in 2014 (about the disclosure of uncertainties relevant to an entity's ability to continue as a going concern).

Keywords Accounting convergence process • FASB • IASB • IFRS • US GAAP

© The Author(s) 2018
M. Agostini, *Corporate Financial Distress*,
https://doi.org/10.1007/978-3-319-78500-4_4

4.1   Going Concern Evaluation
in the International Context

The introduction of the new US accounting standard (entitled "Presentation of Financial Statements, Going Concern (Subtopic 205-40) Disclosure of Uncertainties About an Entity's Ability To Continue As a Going Concern"), as illustrated in the previous chapter, aims to both answer an investors' complaint (i.e. the need for accounting literature to clarify that an entity has the primary responsibility for assessing its ability to continue as a going concern) and implement the convergence with the International Accounting Standards Board (IASB) Framework about the going concern evaluation. From the beginning of this convergence process between the two standard setters, it seemed clear that their differences over the going concern assumption would be challenging. Indeed, the going concern assumption has been present in the IASB's Framework for a long time, having been introduced in 1989. This underlying assumption (IASB Framework, par. 23) contemplates the case that there exists the intention, or the necessity, to liquidate or materially curtail operations when normal operations will not continue for the foreseeable future; in these cases, management may need to prepare statements on a different basis (which should be disclosed). In May 2008, IASB (jointly with Financial Accounting Standards Board [FASB]) published an Exposure Draft, entitled "An improved Conceptual Framework for Financial Reporting", that proposed to remove the concept of underlying assumption as the accrual concept and the going concern convention were not mentioned. In the 2010 final and approved document the accrual basis has not been carried forward whereas the going concern principle has been maintained, and using the same wording, in the IASB Framework as an underlying assumption (The Conceptual Framework for Financial Reporting, par. 4.1).[1] Meanwhile, the first International Accounting

---

[1] "The financial statements are normally prepared on the assumption that an entity is a going concern and will continue in operation for the foreseeable future. Hence, it is assumed that the entity has neither the intention nor the need to liquidate or curtail materially the scale of its operations; if such an intention or need exists, the financial statements may have to be prepared on a different basis and, if so, the basis used is disclosed" (The Conceptual Framework for Financial Reporting, 2010, par. 4.1). Moreover, the 2015 Exposure Draft entitled "Conceptual Framework for Financial Reporting" sets out the going concern assumption, which has been brought forward largely unchanged from the existing Conceptual Framework (paragraphs 3.10 and BC3.4, Exposure Draft, May 2015).

Standard (IAS), turning the framework idea of going concern into requirement, specifies the going concern assumption (IAS 1, par. 25)[2] and precisely identifies managers' role (IAS 1, par. 26).[3] Management should take into account all available information and consider specific factors such as current and expected profitability; debt repayment schedules, including replacement financing; and so on.

The same relevance of managements' responsibilities is now also stated by the international auditing standards. In July 2013 International Auditing and Assurance Standards Board (IAASB) issued an Exposure Draft, entitled "Reporting on Audited Financial Statements: Proposed New and Revised International Standards on Auditing (ISAs)", aiming to clarify regulations and provide more useful information for users to increase the quality of audit reports. In particular, the "invitation to comment" concerning the going concern issues put the following questions. Question 9 asks: "Do respondents agree with the statements included in the illustrative auditor's reports relating to: (1) the appropriateness of management's use of the going concern basis of accounting in the preparation of the entity's financial statements? (2) Whether the auditor has identified a material uncertainty that may cast significant doubt on the entity's ability to concern, including when such an uncertainty has been identified?" Question 10 asks: "What are respondents' views as to whether an explicit statement that neither management nor the auditor can

---

[2] "When preparing financial statements, management shall make an assessment of an entity's ability to continue as a going concern. An entity shall prepare financial statements on a going concern basis unless management either intends to liquidate the entity or to cease trading, or has no realistic alternative but to do so. When management is aware, in making its assessment, of material uncertainties related to events or conditions that may cast significant doubt upon the entity's ability to continue as a going concern, the entity shall disclose those uncertainties. When an entity does not prepare financial statements on a going concern basis, it shall disclose that fact, together with the basis on which it prepared the financial statements and the reason why the entity is not regarded as a going concern" (IAS 1, par. 25).

[3] "In assessing whether the going concern assumption is appropriate, management takes into account all available information about the future, which is at least, but is not limited to, twelve months from the end of the reporting period. The degree of consideration depends on the facts in each case. When an entity has a history of profitable operations and ready access to financial resources, the entity may reach a conclusion that the going concern basis of accounting is appropriate without detailed analysis. In other cases, management may need to consider a wide range of factors relating to current and expected profitability, debt repayment schedules and potential sources of replacement financing before it can satisfy itself that the going concern basis is appropriate" (IAS 1, par. 26).

guarantee the entity's ability to continue as a going concern should be required in the auditor's report whether or not a material uncertainty has been identified?" Numerous (i.e. 138) answers were received from individuals, auditors, regulating bodies, or companies. Specifically, all "Big Four" answered positively to the first point of question 9 even if declaring some concerns on its possible misinterpretation by users of the financial statements and expressing the need to adopt the same terminologies for both IAASB's and IASB's standards. As for the second part of question 9, answers raised some concerns on the meaning of material uncertainties. Finally, question 10 elicited a wider variety of opinion than the other questions. In particular, PricewaterhouseCoopers proposed an amended wording as follows: "it is not possible for any party, including the auditor, to guarantee going concern", because "not all future events or conditions can be predicted". While Ernst & Young did not agree with the statement in question 10 because auditors' and management's responsibilities are ambiguous.

After considering the answers received to the two listed questions, IAASB issued the new ISA 570 in January 2015. The important change[4] introduced by the revised ISA 570 was a full indication of management's and auditors' responsibilities concerning going concern in the audit report. Moreover, auditors are required to indicate the key audit issues in their independent report. This will require auditors to pay closer attention in performing the audit activities. ISA 570 (par. 9)[5] states management's

---

[4] "2. Under the going concern basis of accounting, the financial statements are prepared on the assumption that the entity is a going concern and will continue its operations for the foreseeable future. General purpose financial statements are prepared using the going concern basis of accounting, unless management either intends to liquidate the entity or to cease operations, or has no realistic alternative but to do so. Special purpose financial statements may or may not be prepared in accordance with a financial reporting framework for which the going concern basis of accounting is relevant (e.g., the going concern basis of accounting is not relevant for some financial statements prepared on a tax basis in particular jurisdictions). When the use of the going concern basis of accounting is appropriate, assets and liabilities are recorded on the basis that the entity will be able to realize its assets and discharge its liabilities in the normal course of business. (Ref: Para. A2)" (Going Concern Basis of Accounting, ISA 570, revised and effective for audits of financial statements for periods ending on or after December 15, 2016).

[5] "9. The objectives of the auditor are:

(a) To obtain sufficient appropriate audit evidence regarding, and conclude on, the appropriateness of management's use of the going concern basis of accounting in the preparation of the financial statements;

responsibility in assessing the firm's capability to continue as a going concern, while requiring the auditors to obtain sufficient audit evidence about the adequacy of the management's use of the going concern assumption. Moreover, in performing risk assessment the auditor is required to determine if the management has already performed a preliminary assessment. If the answer is in the affirmative, the auditor should discuss with the management the events and conditions that might lead to a substantial doubt. In the case of a negative answer, the auditor should discuss with the management the grounds for the intended use of going concern basis of accounting (ISA 570, par. 10).[6] The period of the assessment could be different. For this reason, the auditor is asked to consider in its assessment the same temporal length as the management's evaluation. However, if the period covered by the management's assessment is less than 12 months, the auditor should require its extension to at least 12 months. This new standard has started to be effective for periods ending on or after December 15, 2016. The revised ISA 570 introduces a series of other new requirements. The four main issues are the following. First, auditors are asked to evaluate if disclosures are adequate in close-call situations. Second, each

(b) To conclude, based on the audit evidence obtained, whether a material uncertainty exists related to events or conditions that may cast significant doubt on the entity's ability to continue as a going concern; and

(c) To report in accordance with this ISA" (Going Concern Basis of Accounting, ISA 570, revised and effective for audits of financial statements for periods ending on or after December 15, 2016).

[6] "10. When performing risk assessment procedures as required by ISA 315 (Revised), the auditor shall consider whether events or conditions exist that may cast significant doubt on the entity's ability to continue as a going concern. In so doing, the auditor shall determine whether management has already performed a preliminary assessment of the entity's ability to continue as a going concern, and: (Ref: Para. A3–A6)

(a) If such an assessment has been performed, the auditor shall discuss the assessment with management and determine whether management has identified events or conditions that, individually or collectively, may cast significant doubt on the entity's ability to continue as a going concern and, if so, management's plans to address them; or

(b) If such an assessment has not yet been performed, the auditor shall discuss with management the basis for the intended use of the going concern basis of accounting, and inquire of management whether events or conditions exist that, individually or collectively, may cast significant doubt on the entity's ability to continue as a going concern" (Going Concern Basis of Accounting, ISA 570, revised and effective for audits of financial statements for periods ending on or after December 15, 2016).

audit report should indicate which are the responsibilities both for the auditors and for the management regarding the going concern issue. Third, when the firm's disclosures are adequate where material uncertainty exists, the auditor's report should draw attention to those disclosures in a separate paragraph. Regarding this point an example is provided in ISA 570. Fourth, where the firm's disclosure on the going concern issue is not adequate, the auditor is required to issue a modified opinion in the first section of the auditor's report. This is consistent with ISA 701 (entitled "Communicating Key Audit Matters in the Independent Auditor's Report"). Indeed, IAASB' s project on auditor reporting have resulted in a set of new and revised standards on auditor reporting, such as the revised ISA 570 and the new ISA 701 (issued in 2015). This standard is applied to the audit of all listed entities to determine those matters, which must be regarded as "key audit matters". This term (i.e. "key audit matters") is defined in ISA 701 as "those matters that, in the auditor's professional judgment, were of most significance in the audit of the financial statements of the current period. Key audit matters are selected from matters communicated with those charged with governance" (ISA 701, par. 8).

Summarizing, this paragraph examines the maintenance of the underlying going concern assumption in the IASB Framework and its statement in IAS 1 (entitled "Presentation of financial statements") that also specifies the managers' role (IAS 1, par. 26). A precise indication of management and auditors' responsibilities about going concern is also provided in ISA 570 (issued in 2015), in spite of the doubts that emerged after its initial Exposure Draft in 2013.

4.2   FASB and IASB Convergence in Going Concern Evaluation

After having considered US (in the previous chapter) and international (in the previous paragraph) standards, the purpose of this paragraph is to illustrate the evolution of the combined efforts of FASB and IASB in the process of convergence about going concern evaluation. Before analysing going concern in depth, it is worth emphasizing that the term "harmonization" was coined before that of "convergence". The first originated after the World War II with the intent of economic integration and related increases in cross-border capital flows. In 1973, the term "convergence" replaced "harmonization". It was coined by the International Accounting

Standards Committee (IASC) which was the first standards-setting body, aiming to create a single accounting language around the world (Pacter 2014). In 2001, IASC became an independent standard setter and evolved into the IASB. The increasing pressure for a single set of rules is a normal consequence of the accelerating integration of the world economy (Schipper 2005; Rezaee et al. 2010). Convergence will meet the needs of drafters and users worldwide helping them to an easier evaluation no matter what set of standards is used (Ohlgart and Ernst 2011). In May 2017, the IFRS Foundation published an update of 150 jurisdictions profiled around the world: 126 of them require IFRS for all or most domestic publicly accountable firms, while 13 (of 150) require IFRS just for some of their domestic publicly accountable firms. Instead, the remaining (only 11) jurisdictions do not require nor permit the use of IFRS to their domestic publicly accountable entity (Pacter 2016). In addition, there are some other countries which are considering the possibility of IFRS adoption. These are the US, Japan, India, Russia, Malaysia, and Colombia. The abovementioned IFRS and US GAAP were both considered to be comprehensive frameworks, but in recent years, after the US accounting scandals, IFRS gained more public consensus. The main difference between IFRS and US GAAP is that the former set of standards is a principle-based accounting system; therefore, it specifies broader requirements implying more judgement in its application (Barth et al. 2012), while US GAAP represents a rule-based system. Moreover, IFRS do not include as many accounting standards as US GAAP and they are less prescriptive (Angeloni 2016). Under IFRS, accountants are forced to apply their professional judgement instead of following only the letter of the rules (as in US GAAP).

In the last few years, many areas of difference between IASB's and FASB's accounting standards have been eliminated, but some projects are still under discussion[7] (Hail et al. 2010; Wang 2014). In particular, the focus here is on going concern evaluation and the alignment of the standards issued by the two boards (FASB and IASB) in order to both answer investors' complaints (as explained in the previous chapter) and establish a

---

[7] A convergence in the near future is still unlikely. There are evident differences in new standards, such as the financial instrument standard (ASC 825 or IFRS 9). Specifically, IASB issued IFRS 9, *Financial Instruments*, which takes effect for annual periods beginning on or after January 1, 2018. The IASB and FASB worked for years to converge about financial instrument matters, but, at the moment, their efforts seem unsuccessful.

single international going concern basis. This issue has been traditionally viewed in quite different ways by the two boards. The part of the project dealing with going concern was included in the IASB and FASB process of convergence undertaken after their joint meeting in September 2002 where the US FASB and the IASB issued the Norwalk Agreement. From the beginning of the convergence process between the two standard setters, it was evident that converging the different attitudes to the going concern assumption would be particularly challenging: an entirely new going concern statement (issued by FASB) appeared as the only solution to overcome their differences. Indeed, the going concern assumption's journey into US standards has been peculiar, as described in the previous chapter, and also from long before the IASB–FASB convergence process: it really started in the seventeenth century (Table 4.1).

Table 4.1 Chronology of the going concern assumption in the US context

Date	Event
1620	The going concern concept is outlined by the economist John R. Commons because of a 1620 lawsuit (Mitchell 1924).
1892	Lawrence R. Dicksee introduces the concept of the going concern (Storey 1959) in his book entitled *Auditing: A Practical Manual for Auditors.*
1909	Henry Rand Hatfield, prominent American accounting academic (Burns and Coffman 1976), highlights the going concern assumption (Storey 1959; Hahn 2011) in his books (1909, 1927, 1938).[a]
1953	The American Institute of Accountants publishes Accounting Research Bulletin 43, entitled *Restatement and Revision of Accounting Research Bulletins.* It includes the going concern assumption (Chap. 3, Section A, *Current Assets and Current Liabilities*).
1961	American Institute of Certified Public Accountants (AICPA) issues Accounting Research Study 1, entitled *The Basic Postulates of Accounting.*
1978	FASB issues Statement of Financial Accounting Concepts 1, entitled *Objectives of Financial Reporting by Business Enterprises.*
1989	AICPA issues Statements on Auditing Standards (SAS) No. 59, entitled *The Auditor's Consideration of an Entity's Ability to Continue as a Going Concern.*
2002	US FASB and the IASB issue the Norwalk Agreement.

(Continued)

Table 4.1   (continued)

Date	Event
2007	FASB starts the project called "The Liquidation Basis of Accounting and Going Concern (Formerly Disclosures about Risks and Uncertainties)", divided into two phases.
2008	FASB issues an Exposure Draft, entitled "Going Concern".
2012	Auditing Standards Board (ASB) issues the new standard SAS No. 126, entitled "The Auditor's Consideration of an Entity's Ability to Continue as a Going Concern", to supersede SAS No. 59.
2013	FASB issues a proposed accounting standards update, entitled "Presentation of Financial Statements (Topic 205) Disclosure of Uncertainties about an Entity's Going Concern Presumption".
2014	FASB issues the definitive accounting standard about the disclosure of uncertainties relevant to an entity's ability to continue as a going concern, entitled "Presentation of Financial Statements—Going Concern (Subtopic 205-40) Disclosure of Uncertainties about an Entity's Ability To Continue as a Going Concern".
2015	ASB issues four auditing interpretations about SAS No. 126 (AU-C Section 570).
2016	AICPA issues an Exposure Draft, aiming to replace SAS No. 126.
2017	ASB issues the new standard SAS No. 132, entitled "The Auditor's Consideration of an Entity's Ability to Continue as a Going Concern", to supersede SAS No. 126.

[a]"The present, and still more the future, is what really interests the investor; the past is dead, and the investment made therein is, in ordinary competitive enterprises, of little effect in determining present values or future earnings. The liquidation value is of significance to the creditor" (Hatfield 1927, p. 74). Moreover, "it might perhaps be said that the balance sheet is primarily of interest to the creditor of a concern … The profit and loss statement is primarily of interest to the owner in contradistinction to the creditor" (Hatfield 1927, p. 240). This is deepened also in his (co-authored) work published in 1938: "Another important convention in accordance with which statements are prepared is that the business is a going concern which will continue to operate on a more or less normal course. Everybody recognizes that a forced liquidation would bring about large reductions in the asset values; that intangibles would usually disappear completely; that tangible capital assets would be sold at near sera p values; and that even current asset values would be seriously impaired. But such valuations are not significant facts about the business in normal condition, expecting to turn its assets in the ordinary course of trade. The course of trade is therefore one of the factors to be taken into consideration when applying judgment to the amounts to be stated in the accounts, but this does not as a rule contemplate the forced liquidation of the business" (Sanders et al. 1938, p. 3)

The IASB–FASB convergence process about going concern started in May 2007 when the FASB published the project called "The Liquidation Basis of Accounting and Going Concern (Formerly Disclosures about Risks and Uncertainties)" in order to decrease the differences between the IFRS and the US GAAP. This project was divided into two separate and distinct phases. The objective of the first phase was to provide guidance on how and when a company should apply the liquidation basis of accounting in the preparation of its financial statement. The objectives of the second phase were to provide guidance on whether and how an entity should judge its ability to continue as a going concern and, if so, the nature and extent of any disclosure requirements on the matter. Thus, at the beginning of the going concern convergence project, the objectives were clearly stated to be the incorporation into FASB literature of guidance on (1) the required disclosures about risks and uncertainties that may interfere with an entity's ability to meet its obligations when they become due and (2) the adoption and application of the liquidation basis of accounting. On October 9, 2008, the "Going Concern" Exposure Draft was published by the FASB. The purpose of FASB was to provide entities with guidance in the preparation of financial statements as a going concern and on the management's responsibility for evaluating uncertainties about the capability of firms to continue the activity as a going concern. Moreover, the aim of this statement was to reduce the differences between the going concern guidance in the US GAAP and in IAS 1, through changes in the US auditing literature (AU Section 341). Essentially, the Exposure Draft was the same document as SAS No. 59 except for two points. Firstly, the Exposure Draft transferred the responsibility for stating the capability of firms to continue the activity as a going concern from the auditors to the management. This exception, regarding the shift of responsibility from auditors to management, is based on the identification of "information about certain conditions or events that, if considered in the aggregate, indicate there could be substantial doubt about the reporting entity's ability to continue as a going concern" (Exposure Draft, p. 5, 2008). Examples of such conditions or events can be due to both endogenous and exogenous factors. Secondly, in order to facilitate the process of convergence with IFRS, the time frame was adjusted from 12 months to at least but not limited to 12 months. This change, proposed in the 2008 Exposure Draft, regards the adoption of the same time horizon considered in IAS 1. It implies that the time horizon, considered in the evaluation of a firm's capability to continue the activity as a going concern, shifts from the maximum of 12 months beyond the date of the financial statements (AU Section 341) to "at least, but not limited to, 12 months from the end of the reporting period". Because of this introduction, the events taking place after the reporting period should be taken into consideration also in the US annual accounts, as internationally established by IAS 10 (entitled "Events after the reporting period"). The respondents to the 2008 Exposure Draft complained that the use of some terminology, such as going concern and substantial doubt, should have been clarified. In addition, some respondents were doubtful regarding the indefinite nature of the proposed time horizon and the guidance in evaluating all available information about the future. Others complained about the absence of indications of disclosures contained in the auditing literature when an auditor's initial substantial doubt concern is alleviated because of management's plans. Finally, some respondents pointed out the absence of guidance on how and when to prepare financial statements using the liquidation basis of accounting. After this feedback from the public, the objectives, so clearly defined and explained at the beginning of the project, were first downsized (in 2010) and then postponed (in 2011 and 2012) to a future project. Firstly, on December 1, 2010, the FASB stated the management responsibility only in a specific case: it decided that management would update its assessment of the entity's ability to meet its obligations as they become due if a subsequent event that significantly affects management's assessment occurs before the financial statements are issued, or are available to be issued. The time horizon for the reassessment would be extended to include the foreseeable future beginning as of the date of the subsequent event. The determination of whether the related disclosures are required would be based on that updated assessment. The entity would still be required to apply the guidance in Topic 855, Subsequent Events, for recognition and disclosure of specified subsequent events (*Subsequent Events*). Secondly, on October 26, 2011, the FASB postponed making a decision about whether the management of an entity, as opposed to its outside accountants, should have primary responsibility for generating the going concern assessment. Lastly, on January 11, 2012, the FASB decided not to require that management of an entity assess whether there is substantial doubt about the entity's ability to continue as a going concern because a majority of FASB members observed that such a requirement would be difficult to apply and not necessarily beneficial for the users of financial statements.

In the end, after protracted uncertainty, in 2013, the FASB issued a proposed statement entitled "Presentation of Financial Statements (Topic

205)—Disclosure of Uncertainties about an Entity's Going Concern Presumption". The "going concern presumption" has been defined by the FASB as the ability of an entity to continue on its activity "such that it will be able to realize its assets and meet its obligations in the ordinary course of business". The proposed statement tackles some issues that first emerged in SAS 59 and later in the 2008 Exposure Draft. In fact, FASB introduced the 2013 proposed statement highlighting the absence of guidelines in US GAAP regarding the substantial doubt issue, in particular the lack of indications about the timing and the content the entity should disclose on its financial statement footnotes, as highlighted by respondents of the 2008 Exposure Draft. The management retains its responsibilities for the financial statements, the determination of substantial doubt, and the mitigation plans regarding going concern issues. It also holds the final operating decision authority. Moreover, the proposed statement stresses the importance of management's responsibilities in the evaluation and disclosure of going concern uncertainties. So, the purpose again is to include not only auditors, but also an entity's managers, in the going concern evaluation whereas with SAS 59 the responsibility was exclusively on the auditor's shoulders. Indeed, the proposed amendments aimed at incorporating some of the auditing standards into the US GAAP. In particular, they required of the management an evaluation of going concern uncertainties at each annual and interim reporting period; they prescribed a threshold and related guidance for starting disclosures; they stated a 24-month evaluation period after the financial statement date; and they provided a threshold for Securities and Exchange Commission (SEC) filers to establish if there is a substantial doubt about a firm's capacity to continue the activity as a going concern. As a consequence, the entity should intensify its disclosure when it is more likely than not that the entity will *not* be capable of meeting its obligations within 12 months, or when the entity is known to be, or likely to become, powerless to satisfy its obligations within the 24 months which follow the financial reporting date. Afterwards, the FASB defines the contents that should be disclosed in *the footnotes* of the financial report. These descriptions concern five main issues: the principal conditions and events that give rise to the entity's potential inability to meet its obligations; the possible effects those conditions and events could have on the entity; management's evaluation of the significance of those conditions and events; mitigating conditions and events; and management's plans for addressing the entity's potential inability to meet its obligations.

On the one hand, comparing US GAAP and IFRS, the FASB-proposed amendments emphasize the management's responsibility both for evaluating going concern uncertainties and for providing disclosures about them. On the other hand, some differences (in particular three) between the two sets of standards should be noted. First, in the case that an entity does not prepare its financial statement on a going concern basis, the IFRS requires it to disclose the basis of preparation used. Instead, under US GAAP, an entity uses the going concern presumption until the liquidation is imminent, when the basis of preparation follows the Subtopic 205-30 ("Liquidation Basis of Accounting"). Second, in IFRS there is just one threshold for disclosure of going concern uncertainties; instead, there are two thresholds under US GAAP (one regarding the start of going concern uncertainties for all organizations and the other for SEC filers indicating substantial doubt regarding the firm's capability to continue the activity as a going concern). Finally, in the case of IFRS the timing of consideration is at least 12 months from the financial statement date with no upper limits, while in the case of the US GAAP proposal the period of consideration will not exceed 24 months after the financial statement date. The definitive accounting standard (about the disclosure of uncertainties relevant to an entity's ability to continue as a going concern) considers such differences. Issued by FASB in 2014, it is entitled "Presentation of Financial Statements—Going Concern (Subtopic 205-40) Disclosure of Uncertainties about an Entity's Ability To Continue As A Going Concern". In particular, the new accounting standard defines substantial doubt as the case in which there are conditions and events that, considered in the aggregate, indicate the probability of the firm's being unable to meet its obligations within one year from the financial statement issuance date. Moreover, it makes the following five requests: the evaluation of substantial doubt every reporting period, including interim ones; consideration of mitigating effect of management's plans only to the extent that it is probable the plans will be effectively implemented; certain disclosure when substantial doubt is alleviated as a result of consideration of management's plans; an explicit statement in the footnotes when there is substantial doubt (or when substantial doubt is not alleviated); an evaluation for a period of one year after the date that the financial statements are issued (or available to be issued). Table 4.2 compares the current going concern assumptions as stated by IFRS and US GAAP after the issuance of the new US accounting standard ("Presentation of Financial Statements—Going

Table 4.2   Going concern assumptions according to IFRS and US GAAP

IFRS accounting standards	US GAAP
IAS 1—*Presentation of Financial Statements* *Par. 25*—When preparing financial statements, management shall make an assessment of an entity's ability to continue as a going concern. An entity shall prepare financial statements on a going concern basis *unless management either intends to liquidate the entity or to cease trading, or has no realistic alternative but to do so.* When management is aware, in making its assessment, of *material uncertainties related to events or conditions that may cast significant doubt upon the entity's ability to continue as a going concern,* the entity shall disclose those uncertainties. When an entity does not prepare financial statements on a going concern basis, it shall disclose that fact, together with the basis on which it prepared the financial statements and the reason why the entity is not regarded as a going concern.	*Presentation of Financial Statement—Going Concern (Subtopic 205-40)* *Par. 205-40-05-1* Continuation of an entity as a going concern is presumed as the basis for financial reporting unless and *until the entity's liquidation becomes imminent.* Preparation of financial statements under this presumption is commonly referred to as the going concern basis of accounting. If and when an entity's liquidation becomes imminent, financial statements are prepared under the liquidation basis of accounting in accordance with Subtopic 205-30 on the liquidation basis of accounting. *Par. 205-40-05-2* Even if an entity's liquidation is not imminent, there may be *conditions and events, considered in the aggregate, that raise substantial doubt about the entity's ability to continue as a going concern.* In those situations, financial statements continue to be prepared under the going concern basis of accounting, but the guidance in this Subtopic should be followed to determine whether to disclose information about the relevant conditions or events.

(continued)

Table 4.2 (continued)

IFRS accounting standards	US GAAP
Par. 26—In assessing whether the going concern assumption is appropriate, management takes into account all available information about the *future, which is at least, but is not limited to, twelve months from the end of the reporting period*. The degree of consideration depends on the facts in each case. When an entity has a history of profitable operations and ready access to financial resources, the entity may reach a conclusion that the going concern basis of accounting is appropriate without detailed analysis. In other cases, *management may need to consider a wide range of factors relating to current and expected profitability, debt repayment schedules and potential sources of replacement financing* before it can satisfy itself that the going concern basis is appropriate.	*Par. 205-40-50-1* In connection with preparing financial statements for each annual and interim reporting period, an entity's management shall *evaluate whether there are conditions and events, considered in the aggregate, that raise substantial doubt about an entity's ability to continue as a going concern within one year after the date that the financial statements are issued* (or within one year after the date that the financial statements are available to be issued when applicable). *Par. 205-40-50-5* When evaluating an entity's ability to meet its obligations, *management shall consider quantitative and qualitative information about the following conditions and events*, among other relevant conditions and events *known and reasonably knowable* at the date that the financial statements are issued: a. The entity's *current financial condition*, including its liquidity sources at the date that the financial statements are issued (e.g. available liquid funds and available access to credit) b. The entity's *conditional and unconditional obligations due or anticipated within one year* after the date that the financial statements are issued (regardless of whether those obligations are recognized in the entity's financial statements) c. The *funds* necessary to maintain the entity's *operations* considering its current financial condition, obligations, and other expected cash flows within one year after the date that the financial statements are issued d. The other conditions and events, when considered in conjunction with (a), (b), and (c) above, that may adversely affect the entity's ability to meet its obligations within one year after the date that the financial statements are issued. See paragraph 205-40-55-2 for examples of those conditions and events.

(continued)

Table 4.2 (continued)

IFRS accounting standards	US GAAP
IAS 10—Events after the Reporting Period *Par. 14*—An entity shall not prepare its financial statements on a going concern basis if management determines after the reporting period *either that it intends to liquidate the entity or to cease trading, or that it has no realistic alternative but to do so.* *Par. 15*—Deterioration in operating results and financial position after the reporting period may indicate a need to consider whether the going concern assumption is still appropriate. If the going concern assumption is no longer appropriate, the effect is so pervasive that this Standard requires a fundamental change in the basis of accounting, rather than an adjustment to the amounts recognized within the original basis of accounting.	*Presentation of Financial Statement (Topic 205)—Liquidation Basis of Accounting* *Par. 205-30-25-1* An entity shall prepare financial statements in accordance with the requirements of this Subtopic when *liquidation is imminent* unless the liquidation follows a plan for liquidation that was specified in the entity's governing documents at the entity's inception.

Concern (Subtopic 205-40) Disclosure of Uncertainties about an Entity's Ability To Continue As A Going Concern") in 2014.

The new US accounting standard states that both quantitative and qualitative information should be considered by the management in order to evaluate the "substantial doubt" appropriately. Such evaluation is based on "relevant conditions and events known and reasonably knowable" (par. 205-40-50-5). The introduction of the further term "reasonably knowable" highlights that an entity should make a reasonable effort to identify conditions that may not be readily known, but that could be identified without undue cost and effort. In particular management should evaluate the following four (not exhaustive) issues: the entity's current financial position, including its current liquid resources (for instance, available cash and access to credit); both conditional and unconditional obligations due or anticipated in the next year (whether or not they are recognized in the financial statement); funds necessary to maintain operations with attention to the entity's current financial position, its obligations, and expected cash flow regarding the next year; other conditions (already included in the 2008 Exposure Draft) to be considered in aggregate with the previous ones. When an entity is in a position in which the events and conditions considered in the aggregate suggest that the entity might be able to meet its obligations within one year after the date of the reporting period, management should consider plans to moderate the consequences of such conditions and events. Such mitigating effects of management's plans are considered if it is probable that they will be effectively implemented and if it is probable that they will be able to mitigate events and conditions which caused the substantial doubt about the capability of firms to continue the activity as a going concern. The standard does not provide a definition of "management plan" but does furnish some examples that may be implemented in order to alleviate the conditions that caused the substantial doubt. For instance, plans to dispose of an asset or business considering all the limitations for the disposal; plans to borrow money or restructure debt (the factors to consider in this case are the availability and terms of new or existing debt, existing guarantees, commitments, and subordination clauses); plans to increase ownership equity (focusing on the feasibility of raising additional capital from affiliates or other investors or trying to reduce current dividends); plans to reduce or delay expenditure (evaluating the feasibility of plans to reduce indirect costs or expenditure, to postpone research or maintenance costs, or to lease instead of purchase, as illustrated in the paragraph 205-40-55-3 of the new 2014 accounting standard). On the one hand, where the substantial doubt is not alleviated despite management's plans, the entity should disclose in the footnotes a statement communicating the substantial doubt about the firm's capability of continuing its activity as a going concern within one year after the date that the financial statements are issued. The entity, however, should not omit any of the information outlined before. On the other hand, if substantial doubt is identified but alleviated by the management's plans, the company should disclose in the footnotes the conditions or events that caused the substantial doubt before the consideration of the management's plans. The company should then provide information about the significance of those conditions or events on its ability to meet its obligation. Finally, the company should indicate the management's plans that alleviated the substantial doubt.

4.3   CONCLUSION

This chapter compares the evolution of going concern assumptions, examines the implications of the convergence project implemented by IASB and FASB, and analyses the latest statements. The convergence over going concern was promoted by the FASB accounting project entitled "The Liquidation Basis of Accounting and Going Concern (Formerly Disclosures about Risks and Uncertainties)". It was divided into two phases: the first was about the liquidation basis of accounting; the second had the objectives of providing guidance on whether and how an entity should judge its ability to continue as a going concern and, if so, the nature and extent of any disclosure requirements to that effect. The FASB met the requirements of this second phase by issuing a going concern Exposure Draft in 2008, a proposed accounting standards update in 2013, and a new accounting standard in 2014. This new accounting standard incorporates and (partially) revises some principles already adopted in US auditing standards, defines "substantial doubt", and depicts the decision process to follow for evaluating whether there is substantial doubt about an entity's ability to continue as a going concern and determining related disclosure requirements. In particular, it states management's responsibility for evaluating an entity's ability to meet its obligations. Such evaluation is based on both quantitative and qualitative information about both known and reasonably knowable conditions and events. This seems a notable step forward towards the convergence of US and international standards, in spite of the main difference between IFRS and US GAAP. Traditionally, the former represents a principle-based accounting system, includes fewer accounting standards, and requires flexibility and professional judgement for application. The second represents a rule-based system. For this reason, there is an expectation that auditors' fees of US listed companies using IFRS will be higher, because of the auditor's greater required effort. The adoption of a framework more principle-based could lead to higher litigation costs since less guidance could lead managements to make opportunistic interpretations and judgements (Li and Yang 2015). Additionally, since auditors are charged with a higher engagement risk, they could be more inclined to issue going concern opinions (Chen and Church 1992; Krishnan and Krishnan 1996). The verification (also empirical) of these risks may represent a possible development for future research together with the other future trends discussed in the next chapter.

BIBLIOGRAPHY

Angeloni, S. (2016). Cautiousness on convergence of accounting standards across countries. *Corporate Communications: An International Journal, 21*(2), 246–267.

Barth, M. E., Landsman, W. R., Lang, M., & Williams, C. (2012). Are IFRS-based and US GAAP-based accounting amounts comparable? *Journal of Accounting and Economics, 54*(1), 68–93.

Burns, T. J., & Coffman, E. N. (1976). The Accounting Hall of Fame: A profile of the members. *Journal of Accounting Research, 14*, 342–347.

Chen, K. C., & Church, B. K. (1992). Default on debt obligations and the issuance of going-concern opinions. *Auditing, 11*(2), 30.

Dicksee, L. (1892). *Auditing: A practical manual for auditors. VIII-305*. Gee & Co. Pub.

Financial Accounting Standards Board (FASB). (2014). Presentation of financial statements—Going concern (Subtopic 205-40): Disclosure of uncertainties about an entity's ability to continue as a going concern. *Accounting Standards Update (ASU) No. 2014–15*. Norwalk, CT: Author.

Hahn, W. (2011). The going-concern assumption: Its journey into GAAP. *The CPA Journal, 81*(2), 26.

Hail, L., Leuz, C., & Wysocki, P. (2010). Global accounting convergence and the potential adoption of IFRS by the US (Part I): Conceptual underpinnings and economic analysis. *Accounting Horizons, 24*(3), 355–394.

Hatfield, H. R. (1909). *Modern accounting, its principles and some of its problems.* New York: D. Appleton.

Hatfield, H. R. (1927). *Accounting.* D. Appleton.

International Accounting Standards Board IASB. (1989, April). *Framework for the preparation and presentation of financial statements.*

International Accounting Standards Board IASB. IAS 1. *Presentation of Financial Statements.*

International *Auditing* and Assurance Standards Board IAASB. ISA 570. *Going concern basis of accounting.*

International *Auditing* and Assurance Standards Board IAASB. ISA 701. *Communicating key audit matters in the independent Auditor's report.*

Krishnan, J., & Krishnan, J. (1996). The role of economic trade-offs in the audit opinion decision: An empirical analysis. *Journal of Accounting, Auditing & Finance, 11*(4), 565–586.

Li, X., & Yang, H. I. (2015). Mandatory financial reporting and voluntary disclosure: The effect of mandatory IFRS adoption on management forecasts. *The Accounting Review, 91*(3), 933–953.

Mitchell, W. C. (1924). Commons on the legal foundations of capitalism. *The American Economic Review, 14*(2), 240–253.

Ohlgart, C., & Ernst, S. (2011). IFRS: Yes, no, maybe what US companies need to know. *Financial Executive, 27*(8), 39–44.

Pacter, P. (2014). *IFRS as global standards: A pocket guide.* London: IFRS Foundation.

Pacter, P. (2016). *Pocket guide to IFRS standards: The global financial reporting language.* IFRS Foundation.

Rezaee, Z., Smith, L. M., & Szendi, J. Z. (2010). Convergence in accounting standards: Insights from academicians and practitioners. *Advances in Accounting, 26*(1), 142–154.

Sanders, T. H., Hatfield, H. R., & Moore, U. (1938). *A statement of accounting principles.* New York: American Institute of Accountants.

Schipper, K. (2005). The introduction of international accounting standards in Europe: Implications for international convergence. *European Accounting Review, 14*(1), 101–126.

Statement on Auditing Standards (*SAS) No. 59.* (AICPA, 1989). *The Auditor's consideration of an entity's ability to continue as a going concern.*

Storey, R. K. (1959). Revenue realization, going concern and measurement of income. *Accounting Review, 34,* 232–238.

Wang, C. (2014). Accounting standards harmonization and financial statement comparability: Evidence from transnational information transfer. *Journal of Accounting Research, 52*(4), 955–992.

CHAPTER 5

The Role of Going Concern Evaluation in Both Prediction and Explanation of Corporate Financial Distress: Concluding Remarks and Future Trends

Abstract This chapter reviews the main research questions raised in the previous chapters. Their answers will enable us to formulate some concluding remarks about the evaluation of corporate financial distress according to going concern standards in both international and US contexts. In particular this chapter aims at summarizing the main points considered in the book with a view to re-evaluating and updating the existing literature about the concept of corporate financial distress, the types of corporate distressed paths, the prediction and evaluation of corporate financial distress from the viewpoint of different stakeholders, the way in which managers and auditors influence and evaluate the corporate communication of financial distress, the results, and the implications of the convergence process implemented by the International Accounting Standards Board (IASB) and the Financial Accounting Standards Board (FASB) regarding going concern evaluation.

Keywords Accounting conservatism • Corporate financial distress • Corporate recovery • Going concern • Managers' and auditors' responsibilities

The book analyses going concern evaluation during corporate financial distress paths, considering both managers' and auditors' responsibilities. Its intended contribution can be considered according to three perspectives.

© The Author(s) 2018
M. Agostini, *Corporate Financial Distress*,
https://doi.org/10.1007/978-3-319-78500-4_5

First, the book contributes to the existing default literature in a number of ways. Highlighting the time factor, corporate financial distress is defined as a dynamic process: it is a persisting negative situation during which a firm experiences bad financial conditions such as low liquidity, inability to pay debts, restriction on dividend distribution policy, increase in the cost of capital, reduction in access to external funding sources, and weaker credit ratings. Academic literature has traditionally focused on such ex post financial symptoms, because it is difficult to identify the onset of the corporate path through financial distress. Indeed, its causes may be of different types. Considering the traditional clusters identified in the authoritative literature (Argenti 1976; Altman 1983), the book considers five types (i.e. product/market, financial, managerial/key employee, cultural/social, and accidental) of micro-failures. Where a micro-failure occurs, a given business objective has become unattainable and the firm is experiencing a situation of financial distress. If, then, we are to examine the timing of a corporate path through financial distress, a micro-failure represents a reliable signal of its beginning, while its end corresponds to a macro-failure. This is the last stage of a firm's life cycle that represents an important type of discontinuance, requiring a defensive reaction (i.e. a radical change) in the firm that wants to survive. The timing of the examined path is relevant as it may include bankruptcy (one of the possible final events or macro-failures) and a failure process. Indeed, corporate financial distress can be either temporary (if the corporate recovery is possible) or severe (coinciding with a failure path and ending with a macro-failure). Moreover, it may be either truly and fairly represented in financial statements or hidden through fraudulent devices (discovered or undetected). In this way, six types of corporate financial distress are identified. They are all relevant for the various parties who have an interest in the distressed firm. In particular, external and internal stakeholders analyse such negative situations using different possible approaches. While the prediction of corporate financial distress is relevant prevalently for external stakeholders, its explanation entails a deep analysis of corporate trajectories and is particularly relevant for internal parties, not least in order to avoid the same mistakes in the future. Indeed, while the prediction of corporate financial distress focuses on past and present time, explanation considers all time dimensions (including the future). Moreover, while the prediction of corporate financial distress assumes a negative meaning (it aims at anticipating a pathological situation that firms are not prone to disclose), its explanation does not (it aims at understanding causes and consequences of a corporate status to avoid repeating the same mistakes). Newer studies are focusing on understanding corporate failure: its theoretical exploration is today considered the essential premise for its prediction, even if by deploying models of greater complexity and a consequent lower reliability. The evaluation of corporate financial distress is based on knowledge of relevant conditions and events. It can be implemented, first of all, by managers and auditors (through the auditing procedures performed during a financial statement audit).

Second, the book empirically upholds investors' complaints about the need for accounting literature that clarifies both management's and auditors' responsibilities for assessing the entity's ability to continue as a going concern. In order to test such complaints, an important point should be emphasized: auditors' judgements about firms' going concern status should be changed when there are economic/financial difficulties that ought to be disclosed in the audit report, where auditors are expected to judge and confirm (or otherwise) the credibility of firms' financial statements. In particular, a qualified auditor's opinion implies that the firm's financial condition is uncertain: in this case, some limitations exist concerning financial statement conditions, such as an inability to gather certain information or a significant upcoming event which may or may not occur. It is the opposite of an unqualified opinion, which is an auditor's approval of a financial statement, given without any reservations. The latter opinion basically states that the auditor feels the company has followed all accounting rules appropriately and that the financial reports are an accurate representation of the company's financial condition. This book upholds the abovementioned investors' complaint through an empirical investigation. After a survival time analysis of corporate paths through severe financial distress in both fraud and no-tort cases, the investigation focuses on a particular outlier (Sunbeam). This case is explained in depth, especially highlighting the strategy implemented and the fraudulent loopholes exploited by its CEO (Al Dunlap). Similar recourses are identified in other corporate distress paths where Dunlap was CEO before arriving at Sunbeam. The analysis of Dunlap's strategies and exploitation of loopholes in different distressed companies suggest that companies committing fraud view the acquisition of other companies as a second-best strategy, much preferring to be acquired, as selling seems to provide a more successful cover-up of previous fraudulent accounting than acquisition. Thus, the historical financial statements of acquired companies may be a rich future source for the investigation of possible undisclosed frauds. Our examination of the

Sunbeam story also emphasizes the need for development in both accounting and auditing regulation.

Third (and finally), the findings support the need for continuing work
by both regulators and standard setters (both accounting and auditing,
international and US ones). Indeed, the ability to continue as a going
concern must be monitored and assessed in time and in a proper fashion.
In the US, going concern assessment has for years been the auditors'
responsibility, but investors have complained that by the time the auditor
makes an assessment, a failing business may already be on the verge of
bankruptcy or a delisting from its stock exchange. This is related to the
definition of the responsibilities of both auditors and managers in the US
context. On the one hand, the third chapter (of this book) describes the
ramping up of auditors' responsibility after the scandals' season in 2001
through the described Sarbanes–Oxley Act (SOX), a new auditing standard (Statement on Auditing Standards [SAS] No. 99 "Consideration of
Fraud in a Financial Statement Audit") about fraud consideration, and the
revision of the abovementioned SAS No. 59 (and then the introduction of
a new auditing standard) about going concern evaluation. In spite of these
measures, there is still a great debate about the need to restore public trust
and reduce the expectation gap. Especially with regard to fraud detection,
many doubts remain over the role of auditing standards[1] and the specific
mission tasked to the auditors.[2] On the other hand, regarding managers'
responsibility, US constituents have expressed a need for accounting literature which insists that an entity has the primary responsibility for assessing
its own ability to continue as a going concern. This book has emphasized
the crucial role of managers in corporate financial distress, especially in the
case of fraud. The analysis we have applied embraces Cressey's (1953)
fraud risk theory, which is based on the abovementioned three conditions

[1] In spite of specific auditing standards (before SAS No. 82 "Consideration of Fraud in a
Financial Statement Audit", then SAS No. 99 "Consideration of Fraud in a Financial
Statement Audit"), fraud detection remains the Achilles heel of the audit profession (Jamal
2008). Moreover, auditors' responsibility for fraud detection has changed significantly over
time, having major picks and changes immediately after major scandals (Chui and Pike
2013).

[2] SAS No. 99 recommends auditors to ask the advice of forensic specialists. These investigate the signals of the fraud (Silverstone and Davia 2005; Rosen 2006; Singleton et al. 2006;
Hopwood et al. 2012), while the mission of auditors' work is to state the true and fair representation of all material items in financial statements consistently with regulations and
standards. In order to explain the different missions of auditors and forensic specialists,
Gerson et al. (2006) describe the first as patrolmen and the second as detectives.

(i.e. opportunity, pressure, and rationalization), and highlights the role of decision-makers. Firms are abstractions that exist only in a legal sense and lack decisional capacity (Bradford 2014): firms do not decide whether to comply with the law, but rather the individuals who exercise decisional authority on the firms' behalf (Langevoort 2002). According to the personality theory, studies should focus more on key individuals, who are central for any explanation of the behaviour of distressed companies and discovering undetected frauds. The Financial Accounting Standards Board (FASB) agreed with US constituents' need for accounting literature about entities' primary responsibility and launched a project aimed both at answering the investors' complaint and at promoting the International Accounting Standards Board (IASB)–FASB convergence process. This project had a problematic evolution for three main reasons which we have examined. First, the going concern issue has traditionally been considered in different ways by IASB and FASB frameworks: from the beginning of the convergence process, it was apparent that ironing out the standards' differences over going concern was going to be difficult. Second, the FASB project overlapped with rules and standards issued by other US bodies, such as auditors: this was evident from reactions to the 2008 Exposure Draft about going concern. Third, International Financial Reporting Standards (IFRS) and US Generally Accepted Accounting Principles (GAAP) are considered the most comprehensive frameworks, but they also represent deeply different accounting systems (principle-based the first, rule-based the second). Following some notorious US accounting scandals, the IFRS has gained more public consensus: this has led to a US attempt to converge towards the IFRS. This passage has been the cause of many doubts and negative expectations (Li and Yang 2015).

In spite of these three main reasons, a new US accounting standard (issued in 2014 and entitled "Presentation of Financial Statements—Going Concern [Subtopic 205-40] Disclosure of Uncertainties About an Entity's Ability to Continue as a Going Concern") and a new US auditing standard (SAS No. 132) constitute a notable step forward towards an international convergence about going concern evaluation and clearly state management's responsibility for evaluating an entity's ability to meet its obligation, based on both quantitative and qualitative information about known and reasonably knowable conditions and events.

The book's three outlined contributions can be extended in a number of possible directions, also taking note of the most recent streams of accounting literature. Three main ideas are suggested here. First, corporate social responsibility (CSR) and financial distress are both prominent research topics (Al-Hadi et al. 2017). They are still considered in isolation (Deegan 2002), while CSR may represent a key factor in firms' success and survival also worth, again empirically, analysing (Hoi et al. 2013). Second, accounting conservatism represents the differential verifiability required for recording profits versus losses (Watts 2003a) and implies timing differences in their recognition (i.e. anticipate no profits, but all losses). It reduces information asymmetry and facilitates contracting (Basu 1997; Watts 2003a, b). Moreover, it improves the efficiency of bankruptcy resolution, which benefits all of a firm's stakeholders (Donovan et al. 2015). Thus, conservative firms have higher ex ante performance before default (Zhang 2008; Tan 2013; Biddle et al. 2013), shorter bankruptcies, and higher likelihood of emergence from bankruptcy. This leads to another possible (third) trend of further investigation: the recovery from corporate financial distress. It will be interesting to examine in depth (also empirically) timeframes and modes of corporate recovery after either temporary financial distress or macro-failure. In the first case (after temporary financial distress), a specific stream of literature suggests that the choice of the restructuring strategy should be correct and appropriate to the stage of life cycle that the distressed firm is in (Koh et al. 2015). In the other case (after macro-failure), the sample of American companies analysed in the second chapter, filing for Chap. 11 (i.e. the firm's impaired debts are replaced by new financial claims, on the assumption that the firm will be reorganized, as distinct from Chap. 7 where the firm is liquidated), represents another possible way of examining the timing of corporate paths. Indeed, the present book emphasizes, above all, the importance of the time variable in corporate financial distress. The costs suffered by a distressed firm are significantly determined by the amount of time spent in such negative status (Keasey et al. 2015), often making the difference between temporary and severe financial distress. This is also related to the timeliness of management's and auditors' evaluations in both no-tort and fraud cases, with evident implications for both regulators and standard setters.

BIBLIOGRAPHY

Al-Hadi, A., Chatterjee, B., Yaftian, A., Taylor, G., & Monzur Hasan, M. (2017). Corporate social responsibility performance, financial distress and firm life cycle: Evidence from Australia. *Accounting & Finance*. https://doi.org/10.1111/acfi.12277

Altman, E. I. (1983). *Corporate distress: A complete guide to predicting, avoiding, and dealing with bankruptcy.* New York: Wiley.

Argenti, J. (1976). Corporate planning and corporate collapse. *Long Range Planning, 9*(6), 12–17.

Basu, S. (1997). The conservatism principle and the asymmetric timeliness of earnings1. *Journal of Accounting and Economics, 24*(1), 3–37.

Biddle, G. C., Ma, M. L., & Song, F. M. (2013). The risk management role of accounting conservatism for operating cash flows. Retrieved October 6, 2017, from https://ssrn.com/abstract=1695629 or https://doi.org/10.2139/ssrn.1695629

Bradford, W. C. (2014). Because that's where the money is: A theory of corporate legal compliance. *Journal of Business, Entrepreneurship & the Law, 8*, 337.

Chui, L., & Pike, B. (2013). Auditors' responsibility for fraud detection: New wine in old bottles? *Journal of Forensic and Investigative Accounting, 5*(1), 204–233.

Cressey, D. R. (1953). *Other people's money: A study in the social psychology of embezzlement.* Glencoe: IL7 Free Press.

Deegan, C. (2002). Introduction: The legitimising effect of social and environmental disclosures—A theoretical foundation. *Accounting, Auditing & Accountability Journal, 15*(3), 282–311.

Donovan, J., Frankel, R. M., & Martin, X. (2015). Accounting conservatism and creditor recovery rate. *The Accounting Review, 90*(6), 2267–2303.

Financial Accounting Standards Board (FASB). (2014). Presentation of financial statements—Going concern (Subtopic 205-40): Disclosure of uncertainties about an entity's ability to continue as a going concern. *Accounting Standards Update (ASU) No. 2014–15.* Norwalk, CT: Author.

Gerson, J. S., Brolly, J. P., & Skalak, S. L. (2006). The roles of the auditor and the forensic accounting investigator. In T. W. Golden, S. L. Skalak, & M. M. Clayton (Eds.), *A guide to forensic accounting investigation* (pp. 243–257). Hoboken, NJ: John Wiley & Sons, Inc.

Hoi, C. K., Wu, Q., & Zhang, H. (2013). Is corporate social responsibility (CSR) associated with tax avoidance? Evidence from irresponsible CSR activities. *The Accounting Review, 88*(6), 2025–2059.

Hopwood, W. S., Leiner, J. J., & Young, D. G. R. (2012). *Forensic accounting and fraud examination.* New York: McGraw-Hill.

Jamal, K. (2008). Mandatory audit of financial reporting: A failed strategy for dealing with fraud. *Accounting Perspectives, 7*(2), 97–110.

Keasey, K., Pindado, J., & Rodrigues, L. (2015). The determinants of the costs of financial distress in SMEs. *International Small Business Journal, 33*(8), 862–881.

Koh, S., Durand, R. B., Dai, L., & Chang, M. (2015). Financial distress: Lifecycle and corporate restructuring. *Journal of Corporate Finance, 33*, 19–33.

Langevoort, D. C. (2002). Monitoring: The behavioral economics of corporate compliance with law. *Columbia Business Law Review, 71*, 77–117.

Li, X., & Yang, H. I. (2015). Mandatory financial reporting and voluntary disclosure: The effect of mandatory IFRS adoption on management forecasts. *The Accounting Review, 91*(3), 933–953.

Rosen, L. S. (2006). CAP forum on forensic accounting in the post-enron world: Accounting and auditing education reform. *Canadian Accounting Perspectives, 5*(2), 275–279.

Sarbanes, P. (2002, July). Sarbanes–Oxley Act (SOX) of 2002. In *The Public Company Accounting Reform and Investor Protection Act*. Washington, DC: US Congress.

Silverstone, H., & Davia, H. R. (2005). *Fraud 101: Techniques and strategies for detection*. Hoboken, NJ: John Wiley & Sons.

Singleton, T. W., Singleton, A. J., Bologna, G. J., & Lindquist, R. J. (2006). *Fraud auditing and forensic accounting*. Hoboken, NJ: John Wiley & Sons.

Statement on Auditing Standards *(SAS) No. 59*. (AICPA, 1989). *The Auditor's consideration of an entity's ability to continue as a going concern*.

Statement on Auditing Standards *(SAS) No. 82*. (AICPA, 1997). *Consideration of fraud in a financial statement audit*.

Statement on Auditing Standards *(SAS) No. 99*. (AICPA, 2002). *Consideration of fraud in a financial statement audit*.

Statement on Auditing Standards *(SAS) No. 132*. (AICPA, 2017). *The Auditor's consideration of an entity's ability to continue as a going concern*.

Tan, L. (2013). Creditor control rights, state of nature verification, and financial reporting conservatism. *Journal of Accounting and Economics, 55*(1), 1–22.

Watts, R. L. (2003a). Conservatism in accounting part I: Explanations and implications. *Accounting Horizons, 17*(3), 207–221.

Watts, R. L. (2003b). Conservatism in accounting part II: Evidence and research opportunities. *Accounting Horizons, 17*(4), 287–301.

Zhang, J. (2008). The contracting benefits of accounting conservatism to lenders and borrowers. *Journal of Accounting and Economics, 45*(1), 27–54.

INDEX[1]

A

Accounting convergence process, vi, 100–117, 123

Accounting fraud, 50, 65, 67, 74, 79, 81

American financial scandals, 50

Auditors, v, 3, 25, 30–35, 50–56, 51n1, 58, 59, 61–65, 67, 69, 70, 78–80, 79n8, 82–88, 85n9, 90–94, 101–104, 102n5, 103n6, 108–110, 117, 119, 121–124, 122n1, 122n2

B

Bankruptcy, vi, 2, 3, 6–8, 6n1, 11, 13–16, 19, 20, 22, 24, 25, 29, 33, 53–55, 57, 58, 58n2, 59n4, 64, 67, 70, 82, 83, 86, 93, 120, 122, 124

C

Collusion, 34, 35, 55

Corporate financial distress, v, vi, 1–3, 5–35, 49, 50, 54–56, 58–60, 63–65, 68, 75, 84, 119–124

Corporate life cycle, 6, 8, 9, 14, 19, 22, 23, 28–29, 54, 80, 120, 124

Corporate recovery, vi, 2, 6n1, 9, 15–16, 18–19, 21, 22, 30, 54, 120, 124

D

Default, 2, 6, 6n1, 10, 13–16, 19, 24–26, 29, 32, 87, 120, 124

Dunlap, Albert, 65–84, 121

E

Enterprise risk management, 12

[1] Note: Page numbers followed by 'n' refer to notes.

© The Author(s) 2018
M. Agostini, *Corporate Financial Distress*,
https://doi.org/10.1007/978-3-319-78500-4

F
Failure prediction, v, 23–25
FASB, *see* Financial Accounting
    Standards Board
Financial Accounting Standards Board
    (FASB), 3, 50, 87, 88, 90–92, 94,
    100–117, 123
Financial crisis, 12, 50, 87
Financial statements, vi, 2, 18, 20–22,
    27, 32, 35, 50–54, 51n1, 56,
    59n4, 61, 67, 69, 72, 78, 81, 84,
    85, 85n9, 87, 88, 90–94, 100n1,
    101, 101n2, 102, 102n4,
    102–103n5, 103n6, 104,
    108–116, 120, 121, 122n2
Fraud disclosure, 21, 64–66

G
Going concern, v–vi, 3, 7, 33–35,
    49–94, 100–117, 119–124

I
IASB, *see* International Accounting
    Standards Board
IFRS, *see* International Financial
    Reporting Standards
International Accounting Standards
    Board (IASB), 3, 88, 94,
    100–117, 123
International Financial Reporting
    Standards (IFRS), 105, 108,
    111–114, 116, 117, 123

M
Macro-failure, 14, 16, 19–22, 24,
    54–56, 58–61, 63–66, 68, 79–81,
    83, 120, 124
Merger and acquisition, 20, 21, 55,
    68, 81
Micro-failures, 16–18, 54, 59–61, 63,
    64, 83, 120

Q
Qualified audit opinions, 33, 34, 53,
    54, 121

S
Scott Paper Co., 71, 72, 78
Sunbeam Corp, 57, 65, 67, 68, 71,
    72, 77, 78
Survival analysis, 59, 62, 64

T
Turnaround strategies, 18, 24, 71

U
Undetected fraud, vi, 18, 20–22, 68,
    123
U.S. GAAP, 50, 78, 105, 108,
    110–114, 116, 123